CHILDREN OF ALCOHOLISM
The Struggle for Self and Intimacy in Adult Life

CHILDREN OF ALCOHOLISM

The Struggle for Self and Intimacy in Adult Life

BARBARA L. WOOD

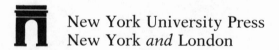

New York University Press
New York *and* London

Library of Congress Cataloging-in-Publication Data

Wood, Barbara Louise, 1949–
    Children of alcoholism.

    Bibliography: p.
    Includes index.
    1. Children of alcoholic parents—United States—
Case studies. 2. Alcoholics—United States—Family
relationships—Case studies. 3. Adult children—United
States—Family relationships—Case studies. I. Title.
HV5132.W66 1987   362.2'92   87-7791
ISBN 0-8147-9219-7

To Phil

CONTENTS

	Preface	ix
	Acknowledgments	xiii
CHAPTER 1	Alcoholism and Co-Dependence	1
CHAPTER 2	Co-Dependent Children: Caught in an Infinite Loop	7
CHAPTER 3	A Structural Approach to Understanding Psychopathology	14
CHAPTER 4	Using Structural Theories to Understand Adult Children	39
CHAPTER 5	The Restoration of Psychic Structure in Psychotherapy	71
CHAPTER 6	Clinical Strategies for Use with Adult Children	106
CHAPTER 7	When the Family Hero Turns Pro: The Adult Child in the Helping Professions	144
	References	157
	Index	161

PREFACE

Contemporary approaches to psychopathology reflect a substantial disatisfaction with classical attempts to explain psychic suffering as simply a clash between human drives for libidinal and aggressive satisfactions and societal pressures for the repression and sublimation of these innate forces. Many of the most influential theorists in clinical psychology and psychiatry today have shifted away from an exclusive reliance on classical drive theory and have become concerned with the fundamental soundness of psychic structure. There are certain semantic and conceptual differences among these theorists. Some are concerned primarily with the integrity of the ego and its subsystems, others speak of problems in the formation and sense of identity, and still others describe disturbances in the cohesion and vitality of the self. Even so, the body of work they have produced is tremendously valuable in understanding adult children of alcoholics. These patients often have great difficulty in making satisfying adjustments in love and at work, but they do not usually exhibit a classically neurotic pattern of emotion and behavior.

Those who enter psychotherapy tend to present a cluster of difficulties that suggest an inability to maintain adequate self-esteem and firm psychological boundaries. Their histories are typically marked by a failure to establish and sustain constructive intimate relationships and vocational commitments, and by self-destructive psychic enmeshments with parents and deeply disturbed partners. Their inability to separate from their troubled families, or to realize their intellectual and emotional potential, and their subjective feelings of worthlessness, hopelessness, emptiness, futility, and unreality do not suggest conflicts between drive and the requirements of conscience and social survival. Rather, they point to specific impairments of the self and its relationships to significant objects.

Alcoholic parents are unreliable and unpredictable. Since they suffer from a disease characterized by massive denial, they are also often dishonest. Alcoholics, and their enabling spouses, create a family structure that tends to be unstable, empathically depriving, exploitative, neglectful, and in many cases, abusive. Such conditions can be expected to interfere substantially with the normal, healthy development of the self and object relationships. The principal purpose of this book is to describe the particular kinds of damage to the self structure in children of alcoholics that lead to severe dysfunction in adult life, and to outline clinical strategies that can lead to the restoration and regrowth of the self in these patients. Object Relations theory, and Heinz Kohut's Self Psychology, are used to illuminate the conflictual lives of adult children of alcoholics, and to devise strategies of treatment that may be helpful in releasing them from the infinite loop of disappointment and failure that is so often fashioned out of their parents' illness.

Chapters 1 and 2 describe the general problem of co-dependence in addicted families and the extreme difficulties that many adult children encounter as they attempt to adjust to the complex demands of adult life. Chapter 2 explores the work of the writers who have done the most to alert us to the special problems of adult children: Claudia Black (1981), Sharon Wegscheider (1981) and Janet Woititz (1983).

Chapter 3 discusses the work of major Object Relations theorists and of the founder of Self Psychology, Heinz Kohut. Special attention is given to Kohut's work, and to that of the British Object Relations theorists. Their eloquent and comprehensive effort to describe and explain the clinical picture associated with the distortion of core structures in the psyche is invaluable to developing a clinical understanding of the problems of identity, intimacy, and self-esteem in adult children. In chapter 4, I demonstrate the usefulness of the Object Relations perspective and Self-Psychology by applying key concepts from these theories to cases from my own clinical practice.

Chapter 5 outlines the strategies proposed by the British theorists and by Kohut for the restoration of damaged psychic structure and the further development of a self whose growth has been severely stunted by early and ongoing environmental failure. These strategies are used in chapter 6 to construct a model for the psychotherapeutic treatment of adult children of alcoholics. Chapter 7 explores the problems that adult children face, when, as mental health professionals, they attempt to treat other members of chemically dependent families.

This book makes extensive use of case material from my practice, and from the work of colleagues and supervisees. Some of this material takes the form of brief clinical vignettes. Four of my patients are presented in considerable detail. These people are introduced in chapter 3, and reappear throughout the text as events from their lives or our work together become relevant to a particular theoretic or strategic principle under consideration. I have sacrificed something in the matter of variety with this approach, and certainly, it must also be said that there is *no* prototypical adult child and the nature and intensity of symptomatology may vary widely from individual to individual. But I hope that by examining the conflicts of four representative individuals so closely, I will come close to my goal of providing an in-depth analysis of the structural anomalies in the psyche that are the basis of so many problems in the lives of adult children of alcoholics.

ACKNOWLEDGMENTS

I was introduced to Object Relations theory and Self Psychology while attending classes at the Association for Psychoanalytic Study in Washington, D.C. I am grateful for the comprehensive course of study provided by the Association and for their educational philosophy, which encourages the open, lively exchange of ideas. My experience with the Association deepened and broadened my foundation in theory, enhanced my ability to integrate systems of psychological thought, and built my confidence in myself as a theoretician and writer. In a very real way, it made this book possible. I am especially indebted to Dr. Rochelle Kainer, a co-founder of the Association, who has done so much, for so many years, to free my own true self for creative work.

Another co-founder of the Association, Dr. Susannah Gourevitch, read the final draft of this text and I am grateful for her generous investment of time and for her comments which, as always, were rich with both significance and fine detail.

My colleague, friend and fellow graduate of the Association, Dr. Rosemary Segalla, also gave the book a wise and thorough read. I am thankful for her professional support for this project, and for her humor and charm, which always make even hard work feel like play.

The Chevy Chase Psychological Center, to be renamed Bethesda Psychological Center in 1987, is now three years old. My co-founder, Dr. Monica Callahan, and I, did our first group for adult children of alcoholics together four years ago, after meeting at the Association for Psychoanalytic Study. It seems that we have done a lot of learning together, about the human mind and adult children and creative endeavor. I am grateful for her knowledgeable and enthusiastic support of my writing, for her professional adventurousness and for all the times she has helped me think through or tough out a clinical or theoretic dilemma.

Many before me have observed that the greatest knowledge is gained through teaching. Dr. Lorraine Wodiska is surely the student from whom I have learned the most. Observing and discussing her work with adult children of alcoholics has been intellectually inspiring to me, and fun.

This book began in the mind of my editor, Kitty Moore. I am grateful for her vision, and for her ability to manage both this book and its author with the gentleness and keen insight of a natural therapist.

Many dear friends carried me over the periods of strain and self-doubt that attend creative effort. Dr. Mary Ann Hoffman, Nona Kuhlman, Dr. Fred Risser, Dr. Damon Silvers, and Pamela Pagliochini—thank you for listening and believing.

A very belated thank you is due Dr. Thomas Magoon, who taught me so many important lessons, several years ago about professional writing. Those lessons continue to serve me well.

The contributions made to this book by my husband, Phil Ray, are impossible to fully recount. They are both personal and professional, and they began a long time ago. Phil recognized my love of writing and psychological theory before I did and made many sacrifices of time and self-interest so that I might attempt to make a significant contribution in this area. He patiently read and reread draft after draft of this text. His wisdom has informed and enriched the final product just as his love, strength, and courage have enriched all of my work and all of my life.

1

ALCOHOLISM AND CO-DEPENDENCE

T HE PREVALENCE of addictive disorders in the United States today challenges mental health professionals in complex and frustrating ways. Current research and theory in this field are concerned principally with unlocking the riddle of psychic and physical compulsion, but the solution remains elusive. We are confronted with the likely, and intimidating, prospect that there are many addictions—just as there are many cancers—and that treatment must be creatively tailored to individual need and circumstance.

As professional interest in the addictions increases, while the literature that forms our foundation of knowledge about this problem expands, practitioners of clinical psychiatry and psychology are recognizing what the "Anonymous" organizations have understood for years: The debilitating effects of alcoholism and other chemical dependencies are not confined to the addicted individual alone. Spouses, parents, children, even friends and colleagues of addicts, may suffer a progressive psychological, emotional, and spiritual deterioration that mirrors that of their chemically dependent loved one. The phenomenon of "co-dependence" is now accorded an attitude of respect and concern in the literature and in the consulting room, and this is as it should be.

It should come as no real surprise that entire families fall ill when one member develops a chronic dependence on psychoactive chemicals. After all, any severe, long-term illness tends to preoccupy a family and create an atmosphere of tension, anxiety, and conflict. Chemical dependency is especially problematic in this regard, since it is so little understood in general, and so badly misunderstood by the lay community and so many members of the medical and mental health professions as well. Families experience intense shame about addictive problems, since they mistakenly believe that compulsion is a moral failing. This shame causes them to isolate themselves from potential sources of support, comfort, and assistance. Furthermore, when spouses, parents, or children from chemically dependent families do reach out for help, they often receive advice that is bad or confusing in that it conflicts drastically with the judgments proffered by some other authority. Or they may receive no advice at all. For these reasons, addicted families turn in on themselves, and struggle all alone to contain and subdue an affliction that they do not understand. In most cases they sink more and more deeply into the problems created by the illness, and are consumed by them.

The dependent individual usually suffers the most obvious deterioration, since chronic heavy use of most psychoactive drugs exacts a substantial physical toll. This is especially true when the drug of choice is alcohol, a substance that is so profoundly devastating to all the major organ systems of the body. The psychic devastation of addiction is equally profound, however, as the addict's available mental energy becomes increasingly organized around the pursuit and use of chemicals, and the need to preserve his or her failing self-esteem by denying and compensating for the progressive loss of control.

The pain of a spouse, or parent, may be less immediately visible, but it is no less severe. Though these unhappy people are spared the direct physical consequences of addiction, they likely suffer from one or more psychosomatic conditions that are caused or aggravated by chronic stress. They may also be physically abused by the addict, who is intermittently and progressively stripped of normal inhibitions against violent behavior. They almost always suffer great emotional abuse from the addict, who unconsciously defends against the humiliation and terror of loss of control by blaming it on the people closest at hand. Saddest of all, the lives of spouses and parents are often diminished, year after year, by a vain, preoccupying effort to control and hide what can never be truly "controlled" and what is rarely capable of being concealed from any sensitive, relatively objective observer.

In the end, however, it is the children of alcoholism and other drug dependencies who are the most tragic victims of this disease. Since their parents are, in most cases, devoted to concealing what they consider to be a shameful problem, and since the medical and mental health professions have only just begun to discover the problem of co-dependence, children are usually silent victims as well. The varied and severe forms of disability that are common to this group often go unrecognized and untreated, or are, in many cases, misdiagnosed and inefficiently treated. Yet, the portion of their suffering that is directly attributable to their parents' problems is very great.

Children, like other co-dependents, are emotionally abused, frequently neglected, and often physically victimized by addicted parents. The nonaddicted parents are frequently too psychologically debilitated to serve as a barrier to the destructiveness of the alcoholic or drug-dependent parent. Children are keenly aware that the drinking and drugging of their parents are threatening not only to their parents' lives but to the integrity of the family as well; and their terror of losing their parents is made nearly unbearable by their recognition that they are relatively helpless without competent adult support. The unpredictability of the physical and psychological environment is enormously disturbing to children since they usually have no chance to escape from the family. Moreover, as children, they do not have the mental and emotional maturity which would help them to reject responsibility for their parents' problems. For all of these reasons, a child's distress over a parent's chemical compulsion will be even greater than that of other co-dependents.

This book is about the torment that children experience in alcoholic homes, and how it affects their psychological development and their adjustment to adult life. The curious silence surrounding this subject has been broken in recent years by the publication of books by Sharon Wegscheider (1981), Claudia Black (1981) and Janet Woititz (1983). These authors poignantly describe the suffering of children who grow up with an alcoholic parent and find themselves so encumbered by parental needs that they cannot proceed normally toward the development of satisfying adult commitments to love and work. These three women have provided us with an invaluable topographic model of the problems faced by children of alcoholics. Yet their pioneering effort should not be viewed as an end in itself. Rather, it should be regarded as the leading edge of a new movement in the study of the phenomenon of co-dependence. It is my hope that this book will constitute a credible beginning for the second phase of this new movement. It attempts to do so by initiating a deeper probing of the problems experienced by adult children of alcoholics; one that ties observations made in the field to an existing body of literature concerning the normal and pathological development of the self and its relationship to others.

I must emphasize that this book can be only a beginning. Since my clinical practice is limited to adult patients, it is "adult children" of alcoholics who are the subject of this work. I do describe the environmental and psychic events that proved most critical in my patients' early lives, but I address neither the crucial issue of early intervention in the lives of co-dependent children nor the possibility that there may be differences between adult children of alcoholic parents and adults who grew up in homes where there was compulsive use of other psychoactive chemicals. Most of my own patients were reared in alcoholic homes, and I have not noticed substantial differences in the problems experienced by the small numbers of people I have treated whose parents abused, or were addicted to, other drugs.

Al-Anon, the twelve-step, self-help group that is the family arm of Alcoholics Anonymous, can play a crucial role in the recovery programs of adult children of alcoholics. I always recommend that my patients attend these meetings regularly. Life in the alcoholic home can destroy one's belief in the constructive, healthful potential of human relationships, and Al-Anon, like a good psychotherapy, restores this faith. Since my purpose in this book is to describe the formal psychotherapeutic process with adult children, I do not describe in detail my patients' experiences in Al-Anon. However, I believe that attendance and intensive participation in this group always significantly improves an adult child's chances of escaping the vicious cycle of an alcoholic lifestyle. I do find that many, hurt and frightened by the destructive intimacy of the alcoholic family group, are loathe to take a chance on any new group, and that psychotherapy must lay down a foundation of trust that will permit eventual participation in Al-Anon.

Other forms of group support and group psychotherapy have often been instrumental to my patients' recovery. Bethesda Psychological Center now offers several short- and long-term groups that focus on the special problems and needs of adult children. I have chosen not to describe this type of intervention here. Once again, most of the adult children I have treated were unwilling, and, I think, unable to participate in group psychotherapy prior to a period of structure-building and trust-inspiring individual treatment.

This book is intended primarily for psychotherapists who treat adult children of alcoholics in their practices. It does not describe a program of self-help for adult children, though it may help them to understand the roots of many problems they face.

The reader interested in developing a program of self-help may wish to consult recent texts by Gravitz and Bowden (1985) and Whitfield (1987).

A final caveat: The suffering of many adult children seems to be made greater by their sense that the professional mental health community, now that it acknowledges their problems, recognizes only their debilitation and never their considerable strengths as people. Certainly, in this book, I am mainly concerned with the curtailment of psychological and emotional development that can be traced to parental alcoholism. Though my focus is on the "pathology" of the adult child, I firmly believe, however, that even the most disturbing symptoms seen in these patients—panicky, schizoid flights from objects, for example, or aggressive assaults upon them—reflect only an indomitable and courageous will to survive the unnatural, unhealthy, and terrifying experience of parental neglect and brutality. This is an idea of Heinz Kohut's that is essential to an understanding of adult children: Symptoms are but the effort of the embattled, intact core self to protect itself from threatened destruction. They are adaptive in that they have enabled the individual to emerge, scathed but capable of recovery and regrowth, from childhood. My intention was to write of the pain that is necessarily a part of this sort of desperate struggle for psychic survival, but I hoped to describe, as well, the qualities of determination and courage in adult children that enable them to bear this pain and even more, to bring it to a constructive resolution. If I have failed at the latter, the fault is mine, and not theirs.

2

CO-DEPENDENT CHILDREN: CAUGHT IN AN INFINITE LOOP

THE CONCEPT of the infinite loop comes from the field of computer science and refers to a programming error that leads to the perpetual and unsuccessful recapitulation of an algorithm, or problem-solving procedure. This is an apt metaphor for the lives of adult children of alcoholics, who seem to possess, as the unwanted legacy of their childhood experience, an irresistible attraction to an alcoholic lifestyle. This lifestyle may include compulsive drinking and drugging, ongoing destructive involvements with drinking, drugging, or enabling parents, and the acquisition of new life partners who reprise the important psychic themes of the childhood home, including instability, exploitation, dishonesty, and betrayal.

Wegscheider (1981) and Black (1981) examined the way in which children of alcoholics often seem to be trapped in self-destructive patterns that are either prescribed or modeled by their dysfunctional parents. They noted that children from alcoholic families defend against the instability and aggression that characterize these households by adopting certain "roles." These roles serve to bring some semblance of predictability to the family and to one's emotions, which, if openly expressed, might shatter the child's self-esteem, as well as the fragile family structure. Wegscheider suggested that the most common roles include the family hero, the scapegoat, the lost child and the mascot.

Many authors have tried to convey the flavor of these four basic character structures. The hero is usually described as a highly conforming, high-achieving, "good child" who seeks to redeem the failing family, and to justify his or her own existence through great accomplishments and noble deeds. Family therapists might also call this individual the "parental" child; the child who assumes, or is forced to assume, an inordinate amount of responsibility for the siblings and the household in general. The unconscious goal of the family hero is to be *so* good that the drinking parent will be filled with pride and good feelings, and be thereby empowered, or persuaded, to stop drinking and become a fully functioning member of the family once again. Since this end is actually beyond the hero's ability to effect, it is usually doomed to failure, and so is the hero. Whatever victories this child may win in the larger world outside the home, the early, crushing loss in the battle with a parent's alcoholism seems to leave an indelible mark on the hero's character. The hero is haunted by a sense that nothing that has been accomplished is truly satisfying, or really *enough*. He or she may be driven to heap one worldly success upon another, in a vain effort to quiet this nagging sense of inadequacy and irresolution.

The hero is usually the first-born child. The second child, who finds that the family has already expended its limited capacity to nurture a child on the hero, may cope with disappointment and feelings of loss by rebelling, taking frightening physical risks, and, in many cases, by engaging in outright delinquent behavior. In some cases, it seems that only acts of destructiveness are capable of answering the emptiness of these "scapegoats," by helping them to reclaim a portion of the limelight that the hero has usurped.

The lost child retreats from the world of interpersonal relationships into an inner world of fantasy and self-preoccupation.

The mascot is the "class clown," who, like the hero, seeks positive attention and tries to reduce the feeling of active strain in the family by creating an atmosphere of warmth and well-being. Wegscheider referred to this child as "a Pagliacci hiding his own pain behind a permanently painted grin" (1981, 140).

While it is usual for a particular role to dominate the character of a particular child, aspects of all four roles may be seen in an individual child, and certain conditions may trigger a wholesale exchange of roles. For example, many a scapegoat has taken up the standard of heroic sibling whose early accomplishments have led to a school or professional career far from home. Further, many heroes display aperiodic bursts of aggression and recklessness of the sort that are so prominently and chronically featured in the personality of the scapegoat.

For a long time, our understanding of children of alcoholics rested upon our conception of these four childhood roles. More recently, the literature has reflected a concern with what happens when, as so often is true, the child in an alcoholic family remains untreated into adulthood. Black (1981) suggested that adult children cling tenaciously to the coping strategies that enabled them to survive the traumatic fears and disappointments of their growing years. She pointed out, however, that these deeply ingrained defenses against emotional experience cannot be sustained indefinitely, and that most adult children do experience breakthroughs of intense anxiety. Black noted that adult children frequently attempt to evade this anxiety in the same way that their parents did—with compulsive drinking or drugging. Of course, a variety of other compulsions are available to help an adult child effect a psychic withdrawal. Some adult children become workaholic. Others gamble, or are driven into deep debt by other forms of uncontrolled spending. Some find temporary relief from disturbing inner tension in compulsive sexual behavior, while still others develop eating disorders.

Janet Woititz (1983) compiled a list of behavioral and emotional characteristics that she believes appear with great regularity among adult children of alcoholic parents. The problems she outlined suggest a general and severe curtailment of the capacity for love and work in this population. She found an overall lowering of self-esteem, a fundamental ignorance of the requirements and workings of "normal" human relationships, a tendency to engage in harsh and uncompromising self-criticism, difficulty in relaxing and having fun, a constant need for approval and affirmation, and an excessive preoccupation with acquiring and maintaining control of relationships and events.

Woititz's list reveals a number of apparent contradictions in the behavior of adult children. She said, for example, that these individuals tend to be "super responsible or super irresponsible", and that while they dislike change, they often exhibit a self-destructive impulsivity (1983, 4–5). Further, while Woititz found that adult children maintain an unflagging loyalty and commitment to people and causes, even in the face of incontrovertible evidence that their devotion is undeserved, she also discovered that many find themselves consistently unable to complete projects they have undertaken, or to maintain close relationships over long periods of time (1983, 4–5). I, too, have observed that adult children regularly enter into, and become lost in, the most difficult and punishing of situations and relationships. They often persist in their efforts to raise a phoenix from the ashes for agonizingly long periods of time. However, they may also precipitously and whimsically abandon these "projects" and these abandonments often have destructive consequences for them, and for others.

The conflictual, erratic pattern of relationships that is characteristic of many adult children seems to be modeled on the relationship to the alcoholic and enabling parents. That is, deep, fundamentally masochistic involvements with alcoholic and enabling parents are often punctuated by sudden, surprising outbursts of aggression on the part of the adult child. It is as if the adult child shifts, without warning, from a mode that is dominated by the dutifulness and compassion of the hero, to one in which the rage of the scapegoat is ascendant. For example one patient regularly worked six, and sometimes seven days a week in an office where she was supervised by her alcoholic mother. Her workaholic behavior was clearly designed to forestall administrative awareness of her mother's illness, and the chronic mismanagement of the office that resulted from it. This preoccupation caused the patient to neglect her own family responsibilities, as well as therapy appointments and obligations to friends. However, this long-suffering woman would also take sudden, unannounced extended vacations from the office. These "great escapes" often coincided with important deadlines to be met at work, and were usually provoked by some act of alcohol-induced betrayal by the mother.

What may we expect from an adult child who enters psychotherapy, then? This patient is likely to present a poorly defined self, whose most deeply held fears, feelings, beliefs, and memories are hidden beneath a rigidly conceived and maintained role that is based on a conforming or rebellious response to parental need. This concealment of self, which includes the repression of intensely felt *personal* needs, may well be complemented by an array of self-destructive relationships with depriving, sadistic (probably addicted) partners who require a masochistic sacrifice of self-interest by the patient. The adult child who requests psychotherapy may be troubled by a tendency toward contradictory extremes of behavior, including a compulsion to withdraw from, or aggress against, intimate partners upon whom she ordinarily depends deeply. This erratic behavior precludes real emotional connectedness with loved ones, and the patient may be extremely socially isolated and unable to function with colleagues at work as well. This isolation may produce acute states of intense anxiety, psychic agitation and depression, and, perhaps, chronic feelings of emptiness, unreality, and futility. Adult children are frequently hopeless about the possibility of substantial change, and this hopelessness, (and perhaps some little-understood genetic endowment) may have lead the patient to turn to some form of psychic compulsion in a desperate effort to assuage inner torment. In short, the patient is reliving the emotional havoc of the alcoholic home and is imprisoned within the infinite loop.

If the infinite loop of the adult child is, finally, to be breached by psychotherapy, the psychotherapist must understand, at a very deep level, the psychical impact of growing up with an alcoholic parent. In my own effort to arrive at such an understanding, I turned to Heinz Kohut's Self Psychology, and to Object Relations theory, especially the work of the members of the so-called "British School": D. W. Winnicott, W. R. D. Fairbairn and Harry Guntrip. All of these men worked with patients who, like my adult-child patients, had been subjected to substantial emotional (and sometimes physical) abuse and neglect during childhood. Their patients, like mine, had lost hope, self-respect, individuality, and much of their capacity for self-determination in the struggle with a parent's severe emotional illness. The British theorists, and Kohut, found that these kinds of patients are not greatly helped by classical analysis, or an analytically informed psychotherapy that emphasizes the freeing and rechanneling of repressed libido. They discovered, however, that these individuals do respond well to a psychotherapy that addresses the overall condition of the self, and the relationships between the self and its principal objects. They found that childhood deprivation and abuse leads to a self that is pervasively split, divided against itself, withdrawn and fearful of sustaining further damage, and ultimately highly unstable. And they proposed that a damaged self can be healed, and can begin a period of new growth, if psychotherapy aims at, and provides an appropriate setting for, the reemergence and integration of parts of the self that have been driven into hiding by the brutal conditions experienced in childhood. The text that follows uses Object Relations theory and Self Psychology to look beyond and beneath the problems described by Black, Wegscheider, and Woititz. It describes the structural deficits and distortions in the self of the adult child that produce these problems. It also describes the psychotherapeutic setting and strategies that can reverse destructive processes in the psyche and promote regrowth of the self.

3

A STRUCTURAL APPROACH
TO UNDERSTANDING
PSYCHOPATHOLOGY

OBJECT RELATIONS THEORY and Self Psychology link psychopathology to adverse conditions in the childhood home that inhibit the maturation of key structures in the psyche. The immaturity of these structures, along with the disintegration and disharmony among them that is the result of ongoing abuse and neglect by parents, makes normal functioning impossible. The structural approach to understanding psychological dysfunction has greatly increased our understanding of the identity and self-esteem problems that trouble modern man, and that so severely afflict children who grow up in alcoholic homes. The unique contributions of this perspective are probably best understood by comparing it to classical notions concerning the etiology of psychopathology.

Freud's Topographical Division of the Mind

The psychic topography proposed by Freud in 1923 is a part of the bedrock of professional and popular psychology. The concept of an interplay between id, ego, and superego is so deeply embedded in our notions about the structure and function of the human mind that it now not only dictates the clinical posture of psychoanalysts, but must surely also exert subtle and not-so-subtle influences on the behavior of a generation of other mental health professionals, many of whom may have had only the most rudimentary exposure to Freud's original works.

Freud's attempt to differentiate a set of psychical agencies had, as an integral component, the idea of a conflict among these agencies. He saw the id as a chaotic entity, filled with energy from the instincts and found it to be inevitably opposed to the interests of the superego, which is founded upon internalizations of parental prohibitions, demands, and judgments. Although Freud's view of the ego was a complex one that changed over time, he saw it mainly as a representative of the whole person, responsible for mediating between the pressures exerted by the id and the superego. He believed that the ego has certain functions at its disposal which enable it to perform the critical and difficult task of assuring the individual a reasonable degree of safety and pleasure in the world. He thought that these ego functions include reality-oriented operations such as the capacity for rational thought, and the ability to perceive and act upon stimuli, and that they also enable the individual to perform certain defensive maneuvers against unpleasant realities and troublesome instinctual demands.

Since the ego plays such a prominent role in assuring the survival of the individual, Freud's immediate followers, as well as more contemporary analytic thinkers, have been most interested in refining and extending this concept. They have investigated the nature of ego development as well as the range of ego functions, and have tried to identify and describe important structures within the ego.

Freud originally described the ego as a part of the id which develops in response to the individual's perceptions of the external world and its demands that the expression of the instincts be subdued and modified (Freud [1923] 1962). Freud also thought that the individual's perception of bodily sensations plays a crucial role in ego formation; that, in fact, the ego could be regarded as "a mental projection" of the body's surface (Freud [1923] 1962, 16 footnote 1.) The idea of the ego as a "projection" into the psyche of bodily sensations and other aspects of external reality has served as a wellspring for certain analytic thinkers who have studied the ego and other aspects of psychic structure and have tried to describe the process by which they are formed. In their investigation of the important external realities that influence the development of psychic structure, many of these theorists have emphasized the *human* realities that the individual encounters during infancy and childhood; that is, they have been interested in the relationship between the psyche and its "objects."

The Development of Psychic Structure: Object Relations Theories

Freud used the term "object" to refer to the individual upon whom a sexual or aggressive drive is discharged (Freud [1915] 1959, 65). The idea that an object can be more than an external phenomenon, that it can actually come to reside within the psyche and alter the condition of the ego, was advanced somewhat later, in 1917, when Freud discussed the psychology of melancholia. Here, he proposed that the "shadow of the object" can fall upon the ego (Freud [1917] 1959, 159); that is, an identification can form between the ego and one of its (heretofore) external objects. Freud thought that such identifications are most often formed when a person, who is threatened with the loss of a love-relationship and who is naturally angry about the prospect of this loss, avoids attacking the object by incorporating it into the ego. One of the results of identifying with, or internalizing, the object, according to Freud, is that the ego begins to be treated as if it is, in fact, the object. In the case of the melancholics Freud treated, this usually meant that the self was regarded with the same attitude of anger and critical contempt that the patient unconsciously felt for the departed object.

The English School

Though Freud's work on the problem of melancholia pointed toward the possible importance of human or object relationships in ego development, Melanie Klein and her followers were the first to treat object relations as the principal determinant of psychic structure and function. Klein's influential group, who came to be known as the English School of object relations theorists, based their theory on observations of young children in play therapy.

Though Klein's work presented many challenges to Freud's metapsychology, she did not challenge his topographical notions concerning id, ego, and superego. Rather, she sought to describe the actual nature of these structures and their relationship to one another in far richer detail. Klein believed that one's relationships to objects, that is, other human beings, begin in the very first moments of life, and that even these very early connections to other people can have a powerful impact on mental structure, and on the character of future relationships. Kleinians believe that ego formation is an active process, fueled by the individual's natural interest and curiosity in the outside world, most especially the feeding mother. It is based on the perception of objects, and is largely a matter of "adding something new to the self" (Heimann [1952] 1983, 126) by introjecting part or all of an object, and ridding the self of unwanted contents by projecting them:

> It is essential that the ego should admit entry only to those stimuli which are suitable and bar off those which are dangerous. In both parts of perception introjection and projection are operative.

When the ego receives stimuli from the outside, it absorbs them and makes them part of itself, it introjects them. When it bars them off, it projects them, because the decision of their harmfulness is subsequent to a trial introjection. (Heimann [1952] 1983, 124–125)

In such a fashion, the infant creates a colorful inner world that feels to him as though it is populated by "objects, parts of people and people...that...are alive and active, affect him and are affected by him" (Heimann [1952] 1983, 155). It is this inner world of relationships, rather than the actual give and take between the infant and its caretakers, that is of principal interest to Kleinians. They feel that one is "no less affected by the condition, activities and feelings...of...self-created inner objects than by the real people outside." (p. 155)

The Kleinians maintained that the earliest (inner) relationships to objects are determined more by the immaturity of the infant's psychic apparatus, the depth of his needs, and the primitivity of his defenses than by the actual nature of the persons caring for the infant. Therefore, these relationships tend to be simplistic, extreme, and fantastic in nature. There is a tendency toward massive reactions in which facets of an object are taken and treated as if they constitute the whole. The facet seized on, according to the Kleinians, will be determined by the infant's predominant need at the moment. An object is good and loved when it gratifies the need, and it is bad and hated when it frustrates the need. The infant in the throes of such a love-hate experience feels that he is dealing with two different objects, and does not understand that he has encountered and experienced two aspects of the same object. Though Klein felt that this psychic "splitting" is due to the infant's intellectual immaturity, she believed that the division of objects and feelings into two extreme aspects serves a defensive purpose as well: Gratifying objects, producing good feelings, need to be kept psychically separate from, and protected from, the bad and destructive feelings produced by frustrating objects. Klein saw splitting as a primitive forerunner of repression. While she considered it a normal aspect of early infantile development, she felt that an excessive reliance on splitting to organize one's experience is dangerous, because each split in the perception of an object produces a corresponding split in the ego. Therefore, an individual experiencing a great deal of aggression toward an object, and thus having a great need to split it into fragments, runs a very high risk of ego fragmentation, or disintegration.

Klein felt that in the course of normal human development and maturation, object relations come to be determined less by fantasy and are guided by more integrated and more realistic introjects that correspond more nearly to the real objects outside oneself. As these advances are made, one experiences less confusion about what belongs to the self and what belongs to the object and begins to perceive the object as an individual who is independent of one's own wishes and needs. Such successful ego development and "mature" object relations were thought by Klein to depend on the maturation of instinctual impulses and an optimal balance between the processes of introjection and projection (Klein [1946] 1983, 303). Though Klein recognized that external reality influences the essential balance between introjective and projective processes, she emphasized the role of primitive fantasy, as opposed to the actual behavior of parents and other caretakers, in determining the character of early object relations. Therefore, she was not inclined to discuss in great detail the factors that influence the maturation of impulses and the achievement of an optimal balance between projection and introjection. She did say that:

> the projection of a predominantly hostile inner world which is ruled by persecutory fears leads to the introjection—a taking back—of a hostile external world; and vice versa, the introjection of a distorted and hostile external world reinforces the projection of a hostile inner world (Klein [1946] 1983, 303–304)

The British Object Relations Theorists

Melanie Klein's work had a profound influence on three theorists who came to be known collectively as the British School of Object Relations Theorists: W. R. D. Fairbairn, D. W. Winnicott, and Harry Guntrip. These men knew one another, and studied each other's writing, but they worked independently. Their perspective represents a much more marked departure from classical drive theory than does Klein's, and describes, as Klein's does not, the kind of parental failures that lead to specific disturbances in object relations.

Fairbairn, like Klein, believed that infants are object-directed from the very beginning of life. However, he also believed that the instincts are wholly object-directed. Fairbairn issued a revolutionary challenge to Freudian theory when he insisted that, "a relationship with the object, and not gratification of impulse, is the ultimate aim of libidinal striving" (Fairbairn [1943] 1981, 60). He also maintained that repression is directed not toward instincts or drives, but toward frustrating objects and parts of the ego that are associated with them. He dispensed with classical topography by claiming that since one can seek a relationship with objects only through ego structures, it is improper to speak of instincts arising somewhere outside the ego, for example, in an id. He saw impulses as the "dynamic aspect of endopsychic structures" (Fairbairn [1944] 1981, 88), and proposed a new model of endopsychic structure that ran counter to Freud's.

Fairbairn was primarily interested in the etiology and resolution of "schizoid" problems, which he believed to be at the root of many psychiatric disorders. He said that schizoid phenomena are characterized by attitudes of omnipotence, isolation, and detachment, and a preoccupation with inner reality. He also said that, "the fundamental schizoid phenomenon is the process of splits in the ego" ([1940] 1981, 8). His study of schizoid problems led him to reject Freud's topography and to propose a model that could explain the way in which the ego becomes a house divided, both in normal people and in so-called schizoid persons. Fairbairn's model is founded upon the idea that splitting of the ego is a universal phenomenon, and that, as Klein believed, psychopathology is determined by the relative predominance of splitting over integrative processes in the ego. He believed that because everyone is subject to frustration from objects, the ego is, in all cases split into three parts. The "central" ego and the two "subsidiary" egos that Fairbairn proposed each have a characteristic relation to objects and to one another. Like Klein, Fairbairn thought that infants typically split objects into good and bad aspects when these objects behave in a frustrating fashion. The infant, who is completely dependent upon its parents for survival, fears being at the whim of bad (frustrating) objects, and so internalizes them, in order to establish an illusion of control over them. Fairbairn pointed out that bad objects have two facets. They are both frustrating *and* alluring. Thus, once the infant has internalized a bad object, he is constantly tormented by an inner presence that both stimulates need and disappoints it. This compels the infant to "divide and conquer" once more by splitting the internal object yet again—this time into an exciting, needed one, and a frustrating rejecting one. The infant represses both of these internal objects, but continues to maintain an attachment to them. Fairbairn portrayed the central ego as maintaining these attachments by extending "pseudopodia" to objects that are undergoing repression:

> The development of these pseudopodia represents the initial stage of a division of the ego. As repression of the objects proceeds, the incipient division of the ego becomes an accomplished fact. The two pseudopodia are rejected by the (central ego) on account of their connection with the rejected objects; and with their associated objects they share the fate of repression. It is in this way that . . . a multiplicity of egos arises. ([1944] 1981, 112)

Fairbairn called the part of the ego that is attached to the exciting object the "libidinal ego," since it is characterized by need and is oriented toward objects. He termed the part of the ego that is associated with the rejecting object the "antilibidinal ego" because it struggles against feelings of longing for, and involvements with, objects. The central ego rejects (and represses) both the bad objects and the split-off parts of the ego that are associated with each of them. Fairbairn referred to the antilibidinal ego as the "internal saboteur," since it displays an "uncompromisingly aggressive attitude" toward the libidinal ego, its exciting objects, and its feelings of need for and dependency upon them. He called the five psychic structures he had posited (the central ego, libidinal ego, antilibidinal ego, exciting object, and rejecting object) and their characteristic relationships to one another the "basic endopsychic situation." He thought that since all of us have internalized bad objects at the deepest levels of our minds, the psychologically healthy individual might be ruled at times by either the libidinal or the antilibidinal ego, but would, in the main, be guided by the central ego. In Fairbairn's view, psychopathology is a matter of excessive splitting and too much psychic structure being sacrificed to the containment of bad objects. It results from real deprivation at the hands of parents or other caretakers. This deprivation convinces the child that she is not loved by the mother, and if it occurs very early in life, the child concludes that it is her own love and need for the mother that has driven her away. The feeling that one's love and need are in some way alienating and destructive represents, according to Fairbairn, "an essentially tragic situation" ([1940] 1981, 25) which incites the antilibidinal ego to launch viscious attacks on the libidinal ego. The individual feels he must neither love nor be loved, since such feelings poison a relationship, and so he withdraws from relations with others. Nonetheless, there is a deep longing for love and intimacy, and the individual attempts to satisfy this longing through a preoccupation with inner reality (internal objects and object relationships) that stands "in default of satisfying relationships with others in the outer world" ([1943]

1981, 40). For Fairbairn, this defensive splitting of the ego and subsequent withdrawal from external relationships represented the "schizoid position."

Fairbairn spent part of his career working with delinquent children, who, he said, came "from homes which the most casual observer could hardly fail to recognize as 'bad' in the crudest sense—homes for example, in which drunkenness, quarrelling, and physical violence reigned supreme" (p. 64). He was struck by the refusal of these children to characterize their parents as "bad" and by the intensity of their devotion to mothers and fathers who were both neglectful and abusive. He found that children who would not accuse the worst parents of bad behavior would easily accuse themselves of being bad children, and he concluded that mistreated children cope with intolerable environments by taking into themselves the badness of their objects:

> It becomes obvious . . . that the child would rather be bad himself than have bad objects; and accordingly we have some justification for surmising that one of his motives in becoming bad is to make his objects "good." In becoming bad he is really taking upon himself the burden of badness which appears to reside in his objects. By this means he seeks to purge them of their badness; and in proportion as he succeeds in doing so, he is rewarded by that sense of security which an environment of good objects so characteristically confers. (p. 65)

Psychotherapists encounter this strategy in adult children of alcoholics all the time. When recounting an instance of outright abuse or neglect by an alcoholic parent (or by one of the parent surrogates of later life) the adult child will assign the "badness" in the situation to herself, saying, "I must have done something to disappoint so-and-so." This dynamic is illustrated most clearly in the case of Rita (see chapters 4 and 6). Many children of alcoholics, of course, believe they are actually to blame for their parent's drinking. This is another example of the burden of badness being taken into the self.

This strategy has an inherent and pernicious flaw, however:

> The sense of outer security resulting from this process of internalization is . . . liable to be seriously compromised by the resulting presence within him of internalized bad objects. Outer security is thus purchased at the price of inner security; and his ego is henceforth left at the mercy of a band of internal fifth columnists or persecutors. (p. 65)

Fairbairn felt that mistreated children have no choice but to enter into such a hellish pact. They cannot reject bad parents because they need parents so desperately. The child always feels that a bad object is better than no object at all. In fact, Fairbairn suggested, if the parents are neglectful, the child's need for them is actually increased, and he is forced to internalize their bad aspects in an effort to gain some control over the source of the pain he feels. Fairbairn found that once bad objects are securely installed in the unconscious, the individual vigorously resists therapeutic efforts to "release" them, since the surrender of internal bad objects necessarily fills the outer world with "devils . . . too terrifying . . . to face" (Fairbairn, 69). However, the unconscious attachment to the bad objects absorbs an enormous amount of libido and the individual becomes preoccupied with inner reality and withdraws libido from objects that exist in outer reality. The withdrawal from outer objects, the existence of inner "devils," and the extensive and rigid splits in the ego result in severe ego impoverishment, intense self-consciousness, and a deep subjective sense of futility and unreality.

Grotstein (1982) noted that Fairbairn's work anticipated that of Self Psychology founder Heinz Kohut in three major respects: the attribution of drive to the ego, the association of ego-splitting with deprivation experiences, and the formation of structures in the psyche based on ego-object linkages (Kohut's selfobjects). Fairbairn argued that a psychologically healthy adult does not display an independence from objects, but rather a "mature dependence" upon them that is characterized by a predominance of giving over taking, as well as an appreciation of the objects' separateness and differentness from oneself. This was also an idea that became important to Kohut, as he argued that a move from dependence to independence is impossible, and that healthy development is marked rather by a fundamental change in the relationship to objects.

D. W. Winnicott, like Fairbairn, was concerned with the early structuring of the psyche, and dealt extensively with the problem of split-off parts of the self. Though he was greatly influenced by the work of Melanie Klein, he rejected her thesis concerning a central role for fantasy in early object relations. Like Fairbairn, Winnicott believed that because the child is completely dependent upon adults for survival, the actual quality of parental care is critically important and has a powerful impact on early ego development.

Winnicott linked psychological health and maturity to the emergence of the "true self," which he defined in a 1971 letter to his French translator as the "person who is me, who is only me" (Winnicott [1971] 1975, xxix). This fulfillment of innate growth potential can be accomplished, according to Winnicott, only under conditions of "good enough" care—care which reliably adapts itself to the child's compelling need (p. 67). If parents cannot respond to a child's need, if they force the child to constantly react to and submit to their own needs, the child's self will not undergo a natural unfolding and differentiation. Instead, the self will be split and there will appear on the surface a "collection of reactions" to the parents' failures ([1955] 1975, 296). This "collection of reactions," or "false self," Winnicott said, abandons play and other carefree childish pursuits in a desperate effort to comply with the harsh conditions in the environment. As Khan put it in his foreword to a recent edition of Winnicott's collected papers, the child who is forced to react and comply is "disturbed out of a state of being" (p.

xxxx). When this happens, a true, "core" self may continue to exist, but will be defensively submerged in a remote and protected region of the psyche.

According to Winnicott, then, the more the parents' needs "impinge" upon the child, the more the child is inclined to withdraw aspects of the true self from engagement with them, and with other parts of the environment, in order to protect this core from ultimate destruction. Winnicott said that the false self is actually an aspect of the true self, and that it might be "conveniently society-syntonic," but he believed it to be inherently unstable and incapable of experiencing life or feeling real (Winnicott [1955] 1975, 297). He found that the false-self organization led to pervasive feelings of futility and unreality in his patients. Though Winnicott viewed the false self as a pathological formation, he took heart from the fact that its appearance demonstrates an individual's ability to "organize an illness" ([1954a] 1975, 287) rather than collapse in chaos, and he firmly believed that the false self serves a critical function in protecting the patient's core being. He thought that where the true self is protected in this way, the individual will remain unconsciously hopeful about someday finding a favorable environment in which to work through the object-related failures of childhood. He suggested that the original parent-child failure situation is "frozen" in the individual's psyche, and that a subsequent environment which makes adequate adaptation to the person's needs will allow this failure situation to be "unfrozen" (pp. 282–283).

Winnicott's views concerning the therapeutic approach most likely to unfreeze the traumatic circumstances of a patient's childhood are quite similar to those of Kohut, and the clinical strategies proposed by both men will be outlined and compared in chapter 5. It will also be clear, as we conclude this survey of structural approaches to understanding psychopathology, that Winnicott's notions concerning the existence of a true self that must be defended even at the cost of a severe psychic illness prefigure Kohut's effort to recast so-called "defenses" and "resistances" as valuable efforts by the individual to safeguard a truly endangered "nuclear self" and preserve it for future growth.

Harry Guntrip was analyzed by both Fairbairn and Winnicott, and like both his mentors saw early object relations as the key to understanding the condition of the adult ego and the nature of adult relationships. He examined the evolution of psychoanalytic theory from Freud to Fairbairn, and offered a wealth of clinical data to support an object-relations point of view and provide a deeper, more detailed understanding of the inner world of schizoid patients. He also amended Fairbairn's conception of the "basic endopsychic situation" to account more fully for the schizoid 's tendency to retreat from real relationships into a preoccupation with inner life.

Like Fairbairn, Guntrip used the term schizoid to refer to people who are emotionally inaccessible and feel a profound sense of futility and meaninglessness about their lives. He differentiated this state from depressive conditions, noting that it lacked the "heavy, black, inner sense of brooding" (Guntrip 1969, 18), found in depression and that it was not objected-related, as is depression. He pointed out that the schizoid individual is attempting to "cancel external object-relations and live in a detached and withdrawn way" (p. 19), and he described several strategies employed by schizoid individuals to avoid real relatedness with others. One of these strategies Guntrip termed the "in and out programme," because the individual fails to make lasting commitments to jobs, hobbies, friends, or lovers and tends to slip away from an involvement just as it is becoming serious. Guntrip remarked that the "in and out programme" is probably the "most characteristic behavioural expression of the schizoid conflict" (p. 36).

Guntrip agreed with Fairbairn that schizoid problems are the result of poor object relations in childhood that make love "hungry" and produce a "terrible fear that one's love has become so devouring and incorporative" that it can alienate or even destroy the loved one (Guntrip 1969, 24). He said that this fear leads to an automatic and fearful withdrawal of feeling at the prospect of closeness with others. However, Guntrip believed that other concepts must be added to Fairbairn's notion of "love become destructive" in order to fully explain schizoid phenomena. He linked the tendency to withdraw from external object relations to a further split in the psyche, beyond those proposed by Fairbairn. He thought that the libidinal ego splits itself in response to bad object relations, just as the whole ego does originally. The libidinal ego leaves a part of itself to engage in a sadomasochistic struggle over attachments with the antilibidinal ego, "while the traumatized sensitive and exhausted heart of it withdraws deeper still" (p. 73). Guntrip likened this "regressed ego" or "lost heart of the self" to Winnicott's "true self," and suggested that, like the true self, it has to be deeply submerged in order to preserve it for a rebirth under better circumstances.

Guntrip reasoned that either the deprivation experiences identified by Fairbairn, or the excessive "impingement" described by Winnicott could lead the child to adopt a schizoid position in which the heart of the self is submerged and there is a general withdrawal from external relationships and a compensatory preoccupation with the relationship to inner objects. When this happens, he said, there is deep within the person a "feeling of being absolutely and utterly alone, or being about to fall into such a condition" (p. 218), a sense of being "an utterly isolated being, too denuded of experience to be able to feel like a person, unable to communicate with others and never reached by others." Guntrip noted that this profound sense of isolation is horrifying when it penetrates to consciousness, and that it produces a hopelessness about change that becomes a particular problem in psychotherapy:

> What the patient feels is, "I can't get in touch with you. If you can't get in touch with me, I'm lost. But I've no confidence that you can get in touch with me, because you don't know anything about that part of me. No one has ever known and that's why I'm hopeless. I feel I'll never get better and you can't cure me. (p. 220)

Guntrip dealt extensively with the implications of object relations theory for psychotherapy practice. His ideas about treatment will be explored in chapter 5.

It is evident that object relations theory represents in some ways a rather radical departure from classical analytic theory. Mainstream analytic thinkers hold that the aim of human life is the gratification of instinct, and that psychic structure, while it is to some extent constitutionally determined, develops mainly in response to the individual's need to mediate between impulses seeking discharge and forces in the environment that require suppression of instinctual impulses. The British object relations theorists believed, as did Klein, that human beings are object-directed from the earliest moments of life, and Fairbairn went so far as to say that the instincts are wholly object-directed, so that what the individual seeks is not gratification of impulse, but gratifying human relatedness.

The British theorists believed that when children cannot build satisfying relations with their parents—because the parents are abusive, neglectful, or both—the children try to achieve a sense of control over their terrifying predicament by internalizing those aspects of the parents that seem most frightening and destructive. These "bad internal objects" are still frightening to the child, however, and so they are repressed or split off from conscious awareness. The "true" or core self is also repressed, so that it may be hidden and thus protected from parental aggression. These psychic maneuvers permit children to maintain an illusory sense of control over a threatening situation, but because the bad objects are installed in the psyche and become a part of the self, they have devastating effects on self-esteem. When the home situation is very bad, splitting is pervasive; and the core self is deeply submerged, and perhaps completely unavailable to consciousness. This further damages children's self-esteem and may destroy their ability to remain hopeful and active in the further pursuit of gratifying relatedness with other people.

Grotstein (1982) in reviewing the contributions of object relations theory to contemporary clinical psychiatry, noted that Fairbairn especially had fundamentally altered our perspective on the meaning of human behavior. He remarked on Fairbairn's substantial contributions to the psychology of the self, noting that he deserves full credit for the concept of a schizoid self, or a self that undergoes splitting as a result of disappointment in object relationships, and that he had anticipated several of Kohut's major hypotheses by thirty years. In fact, the structure of the self and the development of positive self-feeling (self-esteem or healthy narcissism) are now prominent concerns in the literature and practice of clinical psychiatry and psychology.

The steady and intense consideration that the self is currently receiving in the literature is due largely to the impressive body of work produced by Heinz Kohut (1971; 1977; 1984; Kohut and Wolf 1978) as he tried to describe the development of healthy and pathological narcissism and to turn the attention of the analytic community to the "weakened or defective self" (Kohut and Wolf 1978, 414) that he felt lay at the center of many psychiatric disorders. As we have seen however, the effort to locate, apprehend, and where necessary to heal the heart of the personality was already well under way in the Object Relations movement. American analysts who worked to tie object relations theory more closely to fundamental classical analytic principles also made important contributions to our understanding of the self.

Classical Analytic Object Relations and the Work of Edith Jacobson

Some prominent members of the Classical Analytic School of Object Relations include Heinz Hartmann, Erik Erikson, Edith Jacobson, H. Lichtenstein and Otto Kernberg. Jacobson's work (1954, 1964, 1967) is perhaps the most relevant here. She not only made a careful attempt to describe and distinguish the constituents of the psyche and to explain the process of their formation, but also considered at length the sorts of problematic relations between parents and children that might depress children's self- esteem and prevent them from achieving a stable, individuated identity. Jacobson's emphasis on the establishment of individual identity and stable "identity feeling" (1964, 60) as a central aim of normal development is an even stronger precursor of Kohut's concern for the preservation and elaboration of a nuclear self than is Winnicott's concept of the true self. Moreover, her ideas concerning parental inhibition of individuation bear a striking correspondence to those of Kohut.

Jacobson used the term self to refer to the whole person—"body and body parts as well as . . . [the] psychic organization and its parts" (1964, 6*fn*). She viewed the ego as a "structural mental system" within the psyche that contains representations of the bodily and mental self, as well as representations of objects (pp. 18–19). Jacobson linked the establishment of a mature, individuated, identity, characterized by distinct self feelings as well as "continuity and direction [and] 'the capacity to remain the same in the midst of change,' " to the existence of firm boundaries between self and object representations in the ego, and to the lack of significant distortion in these representations (pp. 22–23). She said that the process of forming such boundaries and realistic perceptions of the self and of others is influenced by "instinctual development, the slow maturation of [the] ego, . . . [and] uneven superego formation," as well as by object relations and identifications with the family and social environment (p. 32).

The experience of frustrated longing in early life leads the child to try to incorporate potentially gratifying objects—to become one with them, as it were, by merging and fusing their images with those of the self. This is an early and gross form of identification which disregards realistic differences between self and object. The "most influential factor" in moving the child toward more active and selective forms of identification, and to more realistic representations of self and object is, according to Jacobson, the parent-child relationship (1964, 54). She maintained that an atmosphere of parental love is essential to the establishment of object and self-constancy and healthy social and love relations. Further, just as Fairbairn insisted that a child must be loved for himself ([1940] 1981, 13), Jacobson noted that parents must pave the way for individuation by remaining aware of the differences between their own needs and the child's and making a reasonable effort to gratify both. She felt that parents' efforts to merge with children interfere with the progressive differentiation of self and object representations in the psyche, and thus hinder the development of psychic structure and inhibit the process of separation and individuation. Her ideas about this prefigure Kohut's ideas abut the deleterious effects on the integrity of the self when the child is treated as a narcissistic extension of one or both parents (i.e., as an archaic selfobject):

> fantasies of merging with the child can be observed in cases where parents sacrifice their own needs to those of the child to the point of self extinction, as well as in situations where they either overprotect or dominate the child and keep him passive and dependent, or treat him as but an extension of their own self, ignoring his individual needs and sacrificing them to their own narcissistic requirements. All such attitudes increase the potential dangers to the preoedipal ego and to the superego precursors—dangers, arising from the symbiotic nature of the mother–child relationship and from the indistinct line of demarcation between maternal and self images in the child. The child's fear of separation and his desire to maintain or regain the original mother–child unit are so strong, even normally, that he tends to resist the acceptance of sharply defined boundaries between his self and the mother. (1964, 58)

Kohut's Psychology of the Self

Though the Object Relations theorists marked a path to the heart of the psyche, it was Heinz Kohut who finally concluded that the self must be placed "in the center of the psychological system" (1984, 219). His psychology of the self originated in his observations of a group of patients whose suffering proved largely refractory to the methods of classical analysis and who were characterized by unusually labile self-esteem and a marked sensitivity to "failures, disappointments and slights" (Kohut and Wolf 1978, 413). He found that these patients were not, in the main, tormented by conflicts involving libido or aggression. Instead, their efforts to love and work seemed to be blocked and distorted by a weakened, defective self.

Kohut described the self as "an independent centre of initiative" (Kohut and Wolf 1978, 413) that, when strong, provides the individual with a sense of "abiding sameness" (Kohut 1977, 183) throughout life and enables him to be emotionally responsive and expressive, to utilize personal skills and talents in the pursuit of ambitions and goals, and to tolerate the swings in self-esteem that occur in relation to the success or failure of these pursuits. Kohut measured the strength of the self by its *cohesion*, or resistence to fragmentation (splitting); its *vitality*, or vigor; and its *functional harmony* (degree of order vs. chaos). He found that the self could suffer specific or diffuse damage in childhood, and fail to achieve a significant degree of cohesion, vigor, or harmony; and he believed that the unfolding, structuralization, and crystalization of the healthy self depends, in great part, on parents' ability to provide an emotionally responsive and empathic psychological environment for their children.

Kohut said that a human being, in order to survive psychologically, must experience at least a portion of his human environment as "joyfully responding to him, as available to him as sources of idealized strength and calmness, as being silently present but in essence like him, and ... able to grasp his inner life more or less accurately so that their responses are attuned to his needs" (1984, 52). Parents encourage the emergence and elaboration of the child's nuclear self insofar as they create such an experience for the child—in other words, insofar as they are available to him as "mirroring" and idealizable "selfobjects." Kohut used Giovachini's term, "selfobject", to convey that part of the psychic relation between people that is psychologically sustaining or shores up our self by making us feel understood, loved, protected, admired, soothed. He firmly believed that the healthy self requires the sustaining responses of selfobjects from the "first to last breath" (1984, 49). While the classical view of psychological maturity involves a shift from self-love (narcissism) to love of the object, Kohut insisted that developmental progress must be gauged by changes in the nature of the relationship between the self and its selfobjects. The primitive, or archaic mode of contact with selfobjects, seen in early childhood and in disorders of the self, is characterized by full psychological merger with the mirroring or idealized person; that is, there is little if any cognitive distinction between self and selfobject, and the individual expects to control the selfobject as if were a part of the self. In a mature self–selfobject relation, the individual is sustained, most of the time, by the "empathic resonance," or the emotional and psychological connectedness of the selfobject. Though Kohut believed that the nature of self–selfobject relationships should change in this way, he was adamant about the continuing importance of selfobjects throughout life, saying at one point, that "internal resources are never enough" (1984, 77).

By the end of his career, Kohut linked all forms of psychopathology to "defects in the structure of the self, on distortions of the self or on weakness of the self," (1984, 53) and he maintained that all of these problems are the result of disturbances of the self–selfobject relations of childhood. He thought that the state of the parents' self most decisively influenced their ability to constitute adequate selfobjects for their children:

> it is not so much what the parents *do* that will influence the character of the child's self, but what the parents *are*. If . . . the parents' self-confidence is secure, then the proud exhibitionism of the bud-

ding self of their child will be responded to acceptingly. However grave the blows may be to which the child's grandiosity is exposed by the realities of life, the proud smile of the parents will keep alive a bit of the original omnipotence, to be retained as the nucleus of the self-confidence and inner security about one's worth that sustain the healthy person throughout his life. And the same holds true with regard to our ideals. However great our disappointment as we discover the weaknesses and limitations of the idealized selfobjects of our early life, their self-confidence as they carried us when we were babies, their security when they allowed us to merge our anxious selves with their tranquility—via their calm voices or via our closeness with their relaxed bodies as they held us—will be retained by us as the nucleus of the strength of our leading ideals and of the calmness we experience as we live our lives under the guidance of our inner goals. (Kohut and Wolf 1978, 417)

Parents with shaky selves are not able to provide the mirroring that constitutes a foundation for a child's self-esteem and are likely to become sources of traumatic disappointment rather than ideals of strength and calmness. Kohut noted that the variety of forms of pathogenic interplay that can occur between parent and child are virtually limitless, but he did describe some characteristic ways in which parents suffering from a self disorder might derail the healthy development of a child's emerging self, thus keeping the child "excessively and protractedly enmeshed within the narcissistic web of the parents' personality" (1971, 79). For example, parents may be so preoccupied with their own pursuits and problems that they are unable to provide the child with adequate stimulation. Kohut found that chronically understimulated children lacked vitality and often tried to combat their feelings of inner deadness with the pseudo-excitement of activities like headbanging and masturbation. As adults, such individuals turned to addiction, promiscuity, and other compulsive activities in order to fight emptiness and depression. On the other hand, parents with unresolved narcissistic needs might also overstimulate their children by making excessive demands on their skills and talents or by requiring them to constantly admire and bolster the parents' own faltering selves. The overstimulated child, said Kohut, feels extremely fearful about pursuing goals, and weak and inadequate in comparison with others. In another vein, if the parent is unable to respond empathically to the child's total self, and instead consistently reacts to some aspect of the child that is particularly meaningful only in the parent's psychic economy, the child will be subject to temporary fragmentation in response to stress and disappointment in later life.

One adult child was raised by an alcoholic mother who had been unable to make good on her own aspirations to be a professional artist and a father who was a remote and emotionally aloof scientist. Both parents were intolerant of childish impulsivity, emotionality, and dependency in their daughter and were warmly approving of her only when she was successfully engaged in academic or artistic pursuits. They ignored or punished her efforts to explore other interests, or to extract support and comfort from them when she was fearful or depressed. This girl grew up unable to share feelings of psychic distress with anyone. As a consequence she would be flooded with intense feelings of anxiety during periods of unusual stress—for example during final exams or prior to job interviews. Her inability to express emotionality so compromised her ability to tolerate stress that her anxiety became an almost constant companion. She entered therapy when she realized that she was becoming agoraphobic.

This patient's experience also demonstrates that parents who are unable to serve as sources of calmness and soothing strength for their children leave them unable to soothe themselves at moments of crisis. Since these individuals are unable to check the spread of anxiety in response to stress, they perceive the world as hostile and dangerous.

Kohut believed that in the self disorders, various parts of the self that are somehow enmeshed with the parent in an archaic self–selfobject relation are likely to be split off from the realistic sector of the psyche, or the "reality ego." For example, just as Fairbairn believed that the libidinal, or object-seeking ego is split off from the central ego in pathological conditions, Kohut found that the acute need, primitive demandingness and grandiosity of narcissistically damaged individuals is typically isolated in a split-off sector of the psyche. A pervasive and profound experience of shame about narcissistic needs will cause them either to be entirely separated from the ego (and thus, consciousness) in a "horizontal split" of the psyche (which Kohut likened to repression) or to be maintained within the realm of the ego, but separated from the reality ego, in a "vertical split." Kohut advanced the concept of the vertical split as a "specific, chronic structural change" in the psyche, peculiar to the self disorders, which makes possible the side-by-side existence, in consciousness, of incompatible psychological attitudes (1971, 176–177). For example, his patients often shifted back and forth between states characterized by primitive grandiosity and states in which they were flooded with terrible feelings of inferiority, without appreciable awareness of the contradictory nature of their feelings and behaviors.

Kohut, like the British theorists, viewed splitting as the logical result of fragmenting influences in the object environment but, also like the British theorists, felt that it served a self-preservative function as well. For example, splitting allows the nuclear self to go into "hiding" when necessary. In fact, Kohut proposed a profound revision of analytic views concerning defense and resistance, suggesting that these mechanisms are less a means of anxiety reduction than they are essential strategies for the preservation of the self under conditions of extreme threat. He said of the defense-resistances:

> they constitute valuable moves to safeguard the self, however weak and defensive it may be, against destruction and invasion. It is only when we recognize that the patient has no healthier attitude at his disposal than the one he is in fact taking that we can evaluate the significance of "defenses" and "resistances" ap-

propriately. The patient protects the defective self so that it will be ready to grow again in the future, to continue to develop from the point in time at which its development had been interrupted. (1984, 141)

Thus, Kohut's psychology of the self culminates in a message of hope: Even in those cases where the self has suffered severe trauma, core structures may survive to reemerge and flourish in the context of a healthful relationship.

Summary

The evolution of a structural perspective in clinical psychology and psychiatry has led to a search for the center of the personality and an effort to comprehensively describe and explain both its development as a unique entity and its relations with others. The overwhelming conclusion of this body of theory is that the psychic core—be it ego or self—is profoundly influenced by the character of an individual's early relationships with significant others, especially parents. Through the processes of introjection and identification, others, parts of others, and crucial self–other interactions are taken into the psyche and become a part of its fundamental structure. To the extent that the others are "bad"— neglectful, abusive, unempathic, exploitative—the parts of the psychic structure that are linked to them are split off from the psychic core and from each other. This inhibits further growth and individuation and causes the individual to become stuck, or frozen, in pathological patterns of behavior and self–other relationships learned with parents. It also depletes self-esteem, interferes with the experience and expression of the "true" self, and stimulates feelings of fragmentation, unreality, and hopelessness. This syndrome of complaints neatly embodies the principal complaints of most adult children of alcoholics who enter treatment, and there is much to be gained by viewing their problems as impairments of core structures in the psyche.

4

USING STRUCTURAL THEORIES TO UNDERSTAND ADULT CHILDREN

M ANY ADULT CHILDREN of alcoholics complain that they have little or no sense of themselves as individuals, possessed of a unique self and a purpose that transcends family need. One young nurse, for example, after spending the greater part of her childhood and all of her twenties ministering to the needs of her alcoholic father and her physically disabled mother, succeeded in convincing her father to join Alcoholics Anonymous and sent her mother to live with an aunt. Freed of her massive family responsibilities, she looked forward to moving west and building a new life that would revolve around her own needs and interests. She did not move, however, and found that she was too preoccupied with her hospital duties to even make new friends. She continued to spend most of her free time with her father, who still had much difficulty looking after himself. Finally, she took a job nursing elderly residents of a nursing home. One evening she told members of her therapy group, "I feel I've spent my whole life as someone's maid and now I don't know how to do or be anything else."

W. W. Meissner (1984) has pointed out that the developmental sequence leading to the establishment of a firm, cohesive, and differentiated sense of self is "fraught with peril," that "few . . . negotiate it successfully," and that "some, indeed, fail . . . quite miserably" (p. 387). The earmarks of such failure—as they have been described by Kohut, Jacobson, Meissner, and others—strongly recall the emotional and behavioral difficulties of the adult child.

First, we know that the healthy self can maintain its attachment to, and regard for another person, despite the inevitable disappointments, conflicts, and disillusionments that arise in the normal course of human relationships. There is a sense of continuity and sameness that characterizes intrapsychic and interpersonal processes once a coherent, cohesive self has been established. This stability is notably absent in many adult children of alcoholics, who, as we have seen, are often erratic and extreme in their handling of vocational and interpersonal commitments.

Further, while the healthy self can sustain a sense of worth and value under most circumstances, the damaged, enmeshed self requires constant praise and affirmation from others. This is another quality that is often seen in adult children.

Where there is little sense of inner control and direction, there is also, frequently, an excessive, sometimes fanatical devotion to causes, beliefs, leaders, and partners that seem to offer a possibility of focus and stability. This phenomenon is evocative of the self-destructive, misguided loyalty that many adult children display in relation to lost causes and impossible partners.

Our literature also tells us that a firm, integrated sense of self not only facilitates stable commitments to others but also increases the ability to tolerate differences and separateness from those we love and admire. The shaky, undifferentiated self cannot stand apart and retains a persistent, intense emotional attachment to family members, focusing narrowly and obsessively on their needs, at the expense of personal well-being. Meissner remarked that, while "one of the most important features" of the mature individuated self is "the capacity to buffer himself against the hurts, pain, and suffering of others around him"

(1984, 389), poorly individuated people seem unable to maintain their own emotional functioning when another family member is in crisis. Indeed, they seem to suffer as severely as if the crisis were their own. According to Meissner, the individual who finds herself hopelessly entangled in this sort of self-annihilating relation with parents and siblings either remains in a position of compliant submission to them (as did the "heroic" young nurse described above), or reacts with a rebellious denial of dependence and an exaggerated display of adequacy and self-sufficiency that conceals the conflict and the "faltering, fragile" sense of self underneath" (p. 388). In other words, true spontaneity and individuality are lost as the child is either absorbed by the needs of the troubled family, like the hero, or engages in a desperate and equally self-suffocating attempt to repell the onslaught by defining herself through total opposition to them, as does the scapegoat.

Finally, as the work of the British School and that of Kohut make clear, a poorly formed self is subject to pervasive and profound feelings of futility, hopelessness, and unreality. These are common complaints of adult children.

It is the fundamental assumption here that many of the problems adult children experience, including the failure to separate from the family of origin and become a true individual, the inability to establish stable commitments in love and work, the compulsive engagement with hopeless persons and causes, and the severe depletion of self-esteem, can all be understood as the result of damage to the structure of the self. This damage is rooted in the troubled parent–child relationships that are characteristic of alcoholic families, and which lead to severe disturbances of the internal object relationships which form the foundation of the self. One purpose of this book is to provide a deeper understanding of the adult child by describing the specific types of damage to the self that are likely to occur in alcoholic homes.

The Adult Child's Failure to Separate

The central problem may be the adult child's inability to separate psychologically from the alcoholic family and to realize a true individuality. Sometimes children of alcoholics are actually unable to physically separate from their families, but more frequently they exhibit a psychic enmeshment with their parents. This enmeshment takes the form of a seemingly irresistible attraction to an alcoholic lifestyle (See chapter 2). The failure to separate from parents may occur even in the face of abuse and exploitation at their hands. It is a problem that undoubtedly has multiple roots.

First, the developmental task of separation and individuation is always complicated by the child's need for the parent, and by the child's natural compassion and tender love for that parent. Profound love and intense need bind children to their parents and foster in them a resolve and a willingness to suffer great pain in the service of their parents' survival. Children of alcoholics feel, with considerable justification, that their parents' survival is greatly in doubt.

Second, it is also true that many alcoholic parents and many enabling spouses consciously or unconsciously exploit the love and need that their children feel. They cope with the self-doubt and self-disgust that have accumulated over the course of an extended and debilitating battle with the bottle by projecting these feelings into their children. That is, they avoid seeing themselves as weak and bad by seeing their children as weak and bad, and telling them they are weak and bad. The child is usually willing to feel (and act) weak and bad if this will stabilize the parent and, after many years of serving this function, becomes indispensable to the parents' psychological stability. Therefore, the parents will exert enormous pressure on the child *not* to separate. One patient, a talented artist who will be described more fully below, was constantly criticized by his parents as passive and ineffectual, with no chance for success in the art world. Interestingly, much of this criticism came from his mother, who in her youth had exchanged her own artistic aspirations for marriage and motherhood. Both parents loudly and angrily insisted to this patient that he would always be financially dependent upon them, and while he experienced such declarations as an expression of his parents' disappointment in him, they seemed to me to be expressions of his parents' need for him—unconscious efforts to paralyze him with shame and keep him at home. They worked remarkably well.

Finally, there is a near-universal clinical impression that old conflict situations are compelling psychic sirens for most of us. It is as though we do the same things over and over again in what is usually a futile effort to "get it right." The Anonymous programs advance this phenomenon as the operational definition of insanity.

Though all of these forces interfere with the efforts of adult children to separate from their alcoholic families, a contemporary student of psychopathology, interested in the relationship of behavioral and emotional disorders to the impairment of psychic structure, might also relate the separation problem to a failure by adult children to establish an adequately differentiated, cohesive identity or sense of self. The alcoholic home is, by degrees, a chronically abusive, exploitative, and neglectful environment that can certainly be expected to derail the normal, healthy development of the self. Since Self Psychology and object relations theory explore the impact of parent–child relationships on the evolution of the self and on subsequent attachments, they provide a logical jumping-off point for our study of separation problems in adult children of alcoholics.

An Object Relations and Self Psychological Perspective

The "False Self" of the Adult Child.   A common premise of the theories advanced by the British School and of the Self Psychology proposed by Kohut is that there is, for each individual a "true" or nuclear self that under favorable conditions will unfold and assert itself by forming constructive relationships with others and using its native gifts. Where conditions are so unfavorable as to pose a threat to the existence of this core self, it will be defensively submerged deep within the psyche where it will be safe from harm. Winnicott, as we have seen, believed that under these circumstances, an unstable but convincing "false self" will arise to do business with the world at large and to divert aggression away from the frightened self within. Kohut advanced a similar idea with his discussion of the adaptive value of certain defensive structures in preserving the nuclear self of the child who is raised in an atmosphere of unreliable empathy and traumatic disappointment. The concept of a defensively (adaptively) conceived false self can be used to expand our understanding of the separation and individuation conflicts that adult children experience.

In alcoholic homes, the possibility of good-enough care, as it was conceived by Winnicott and others, is lost to a preoccupation with the pursuit and use of alcohol, as well as with the need to conceal, deny, and compensate for this fact. The alcoholic, and her enabling spouse, have little additional energy to devote to an adaptation to the needs of their children. Instead, the children are likely to be forced to adapt to a chaotic reality that may include extremes of abuse and neglect; and very often, they find that they must nurture and support their parents when they are drunk or despairing, or otherwise broken down. These children frequently adopt false selves in the form of the roles explored earlier, including the hero, the scapegoat, the lost child, and the mascot. These false selves are based on reactions to parental character and they represent an attempt to deal with key parental failures. They both conceal and protect important aspects of inner reality.

The false self that is founded upon heroic accomplishments and massive self-sacrifice is frequently encountered in treatment. Though the heroic position is, in Winnicott's words, "society-syntonic," and frequently reaps substantial professional recognition and financial reward, its emphasis on perfectionism, total self-sufficiency, and denial of vulnerability can also produce depression, massive anxiety, and a deep sense of isolation and emptiness.

Jack

Jack, a 25-year-old social worker, entered treatment after a clinical supervisor praised his intellectual gifts, but suggested that his difficulty in establishing and maintaining an empathic bond with his clients might curtail his further advancement as a professional. Jack could not say whether he failed to notice significant emotional material in clinical interviews, or whether he withdrew from it, but he had always experienced difficulty in feeling truly connected to other people. At the time he entered therapy, he felt very isolated and remote from others and saw his life as being largely without meaning. He believed that he was essentially worthless to others. Jack had come close to committing suicide a few years earlier, and still had a profound sense of "not belonging" in the world, and of having no purpose here.

Jack was the oldest of four children born to an alcoholic, workaholic physician father and a mother who suffered from a chronic heart ailment. His father's twin compulsions, and his mother's debilitating illness (which required repeated hospitalizations), left Jack with extensive responsibility for his younger siblings. He reported that he was expected to be cook, launderer, general caretaker and goundsman for the family, to excel at sports and to receive straight A's at school as well. In much of this, Jack appeared to be taking up slack for his father, who was usually too busy or too inebriated to assume physical and emotional responsibility for the children when Jack's mother was ill. On one particularly harrowing occasion, 13-year-old Jack was literally placed in the driver's seat when his father got drunk at a family outing and a neighbor recognized that he was unable to drive home. The neighbor gave Jack the keys and instructed him to take the family home. Jack had never driven before, and in fact, could barely reach the brake and gas pedals. He was astonished that he was able to get the family home safely.

Jack felt that the enormous effort he expended meeting his family's various needs and demands was not appreciated by either his parents or his brothers; that it was taken as a matter of course that he would perform as necessary. He believed that he actually had no importance at all to his family except as a servant of sorts, and that if he ever failed to meet their expectations, even this minimal connection to them would dissolve, and he would be entirely alone.

Jack's parents, overburdened and preoccupied as they were by their own illnesses, seemed unable to tolerate expressions of need or vulnerability in their oldest child. They could not comfort him, and his requests for help or support were always rebuffed. If he asked for the spelling of a word when doing his homework, his mother icily referred him to the dictionary. When he was suffering from a severe ear infection, he was nonetheless given full charge of his siblings for an entire evening, and his pain became so intense that he finally ran to the home of a neighboring physician for help. When Jack injured his foot in a basketball game as a teenager, his father examined it cursorily, packed it in ice to reduce the swelling, and declared that it needed no further treatment. Though the foot continued to pain him for years, Jack tolerated this pain without complaint. The foot was never x-rayed until a college coach became alarmed at the chronicity of Jack's problems with the foot, which would swell and cause him to walk with a slight limp. The coach sent Jack to a doctor who performed an x-ray and discovered that the foot had, in fact, been broken and had healed improperly.

Jack's parents needed to see him as a flawless superchild, able to turn in a perfect performance in any realm, and under any circumstances. Their idealization of their son left him harshly intolerant of pain, vulnerability, and imperfection in himself. Though he felt severely depressed during his adolescence and seriously considered suicide, he was too ashamed of these feelings to express them to anyone. When a high school teacher attempted to discuss with him the latent meaning of his selection of adolescent suicide as the theme for an English composition, he was unable to respond to her concern, and denied his deepening depression. Whenever he became aware of the pain of his parents' neglect and exploitation of him, he would withdraw to his room, or to a favorite tree in the woods in order to banish his pain and reestablish his capable, cheerful façade. He never imagined that another person would care to comfort him at these times, but soothed himself with the fantasy that the tree actually "held" him and that he was floating above his pain and hurt (splitting it off). As he grew older, he became less and less capable of expressing emotional and physical needs to any animate object and less and less capable of responding to his needs in any sort of gratifying way. Though he felt completely alienated from his family, he unconsciously continued to devote himself to fulfilling their dream of an ideal and invulnerable child, devoid of need or individual purpose. He rarely sought help for injuries and physical illnesses until his pain became incapacitating, and though his desire for recognition and nurturance from others occasionally broke through to consciousness, his guilt and shame about these longings led him to submerge them once again and to remain aloof and inexpressive (and therefore dissatisfied) in most of the relationships he tried to establish. He continued to pretend to the world and to himself that he could exist entirely without help or emotional support of any kind. His considerable psychic and intellectual resources enabled him to maintain this false position for a considerable length of time. He was, in fact, able to fulfill his family's need for a hero in most respects, and to achieve at a very high level in school and in many aspects of his work life. However, his retreat from emotionality and need for others (that is, his alienation from his "true" self) was not without substantial penalty. It deprived him of the stuff of which real relationships are made and left him isolated, empty, and depressed.

Meissner described the efforts of the false self to comply with parental demands as passive and masochistic (1984, 456–457). Though Jack's behavior may be accurately described in these terms, a child may also comply with an antagonistic environment by erecting a false self that is overtly organized around aggression, rebellion, and feelings of superiority. This is true of the scapegoat, whose brash interpersonal style contrasts sharply with that of the hero. The scapegoat is also quite commonly seen in treatment, and is frequently referred by school authorities or a representative of the criminal justice system.

Ed

Ed was referred for treatment by his attorney, who recommended that he seek professional evaluation and counseling prior to standing trial for an arrest on charges of possessing (with intent to distribute) a controlled dangerous substance. At 23, Ed was already a tough, mouthy drug dealer with a rather extensive following. He was also in a great deal of trouble, not only with the law, but also with other dealers, who were pressing him for money and threatening to kill him if he failed to make good on his debts to them. Before his arrest, he had almost always carried a gun.

Though Ed obviously relished many aspects of his life dealing drugs, he seemed, in many ways, an unlikely candidate for a life of felony and physical jeopardy. He was the oldest son of a successful, but heavily drinking accountant and a clearly alcoholic mother who had been killed in an alcohol-related car crash when he was six, and he openly aspired to the respectable, affluent professional life into which he had been born. He had always planned to give up dealing when he finished school and to become a banker, or perhaps an economist like his favorite uncle. These goals were of course, compromised by his arrest, and also by his poor record in college. Though Ed was very bright, he had done only average work in school, and had accumulated enough withdrawals and incompletes to make his pursuit of a sheepskin seem a ceaseless request. This poor performance appeared to be the result of a penchant for partying and hopeless love affairs in which he was at first intently pursued and then precipitously dumped by one exploitative woman after another. These abandonments left him in a severely grief-stricken and almost completely helpless state.

Ed's relationship to his family had been complicated from the beginning. His early memories of his natural mother were dim and confused. He did know that he had spent at least one terrifying night alone with her on a wild drive through town after she had had a terrible fight with his father. He did not know whether he remembered this incident or whether it had been described to him by his father, but he could remember feeling afraid of his mother.

His relationships with his father and stepmother were equally disturbing to him. He felt that his stepmother, especially, was resentful of his very existence and was trying to destroy his relationship with his father. Ed was seven when his father remarried, and his stepmother had been in charge of his care, including all discipline, since that time. Ed never felt warmth or affection from his stepmother, who was sharply critical of him for the behavioral and academic disturbances he manifested in school, even at this age. Both parents seemed to regard these early signs of emotional disturbance as disciplinary issues, and Ed's father gave his stepmother free reign to respond to them with corporal punishment or the withdrawal of privileges. She relied mostly on spanking when Ed was very young, and he remembered these punishments with intense anger and equally intense shame. He felt she had used her greater size to intimidate him, and it humiliated him to remember how frightened he was of her at that time.

As Ed grew older and bigger, he got into more complicated scrapes at his private school, where he had begun to use and deal marijuana. These activities had a further del-

eterious effect on his academic performance. His stepmother began to use verbal ridicule and financial sanctions
in an effort to control him. Her contemptuous suggestion
that an ultimately uncontrollable craziness "like your
mother's" might be at the root of his difficulty was especially painful to him, as was her loud and frequent lament
that he would likely continue to be a financial burden to
his father for the rest of his life. When she withheld his
clothing allowance and spending money as well, he was
unable to keep pace with the well-heeled peer group to
which he desperately aspired, and his self-esteem plum-
meted ever lower, while his feelings of shame and inferiority soared.

Ed's father never intervened in these altercations. When
Ed complained openly about the lot that had befallen him
as the result of his mother's death, his father reminded him
that his natural mother had been no prize and counseled
that, at any rate, most relationships proved bitterly disappointing in the end. He shared with Ed his own sense of
frustration and failure in marriage and advised his son to
learn to survive by his own wits and resources. He was
harshly critical of Ed's disastrous romantic involvements,
and pointed to each as a confirmation of his world view
and as fresh evidence of his son's inability to meet the
challenge of survival through total self-sufficiency.

The philosophy espoused by his father seemed to Ed
nothing more than an attempt to rationalize the strategy
of avoidance and withdrawal the father had practiced most
of his life. Ed was extremely bitter about his father's failure
to save his natural mother from her alcoholism, and he was
angry as well about his father's retreat from his responsibility to protect Ed from his stepmother. He therefore received his father's observations about life with rageful
denunciations of the man.

The uncovering work of therapy however, revealed that
Ed mostly believed the things his father and mother either
said openly about him or implied. He felt that he was a
dependent, inadequate wimp, who would probably wind
up a crazy drunk like his mother. While such feelings

emerged in therapy, and broke through on those occasions when he faced the loss of a girlfriend, they were completely unavailable to him in that portion of his life, and self, that was devoted to dealing drugs. In this realm, he was supremely tough, effective, and self-confident. He thrilled at the opportunity to wave a revolver at his estranged partners in crime, temporarily released from the paralyzing shame and terror he had felt at the hands of his mother and stepmother. The financial spoils gave the lie to the overwhelming powerlessness he felt with his parents and he reveled in the supplications and attentions of hopeful, sometimes desperate junkies, never consciously recognizing his own lonely craving in their eyes.

These case studies make clear that the scapegoat is often kin to the hero in a psychological, as well a fraternal sense. The scapegoat, like the hero, is frequently characterized by a vertical split in the psyche that effectively denies and conceals the vulnerability, hurt, and need that are such a vivid part of the true self but which are unacceptable to the troubled and overwhelmed parents. Both self-types suffer from critically low self-esteem. While the hero may be more consistently conscious of a deficit in self-esteem, however, the scapegoat usually banishes feelings of self-doubt and self-depreciation to the unconscious realm of the true self. It is important to understand that the false self is a largely unconscious device, and that, much as active alcoholics remain deluded as to the dimensions and destructive impact of their drinking problems, children of alcoholics remain grossly unaware of many aspects of their inner experience, as well as the fact of their estrangement from it.

The Internalized Bad Object.   The preceding material describes how the self of the adult child is powerfully affected by what the alcoholic and the enabling spouse desperately need their children to be. It is clear that the adult child's self suffers considerable damage and distortion as it tries to respond to this desperate need. This damage substantially hinders the process of separation and individuation, since it involves the burial of many "true" aspects of character that would ordinarily instill in one a feeling of wholeness and reality, and serve to distinguish self from other. With the true self in hiding, the adult child remains, as Kohut puts it, "enmeshed within the narcissistic web of the parents' personality," or in a state of psychological merger with them. While the self of the adult child is decisively altered by what the parents need, however, it is also profoundly influenced by what they *are*, which also impedes separation and individuation. The following two cases will serve as a basis for discussion of this phenomenon:

Rita

Rita was a 28-year-old recovering alcoholic and heroin addict. She was the daughter of an alcoholic, physically abusive mother. Rita worked in her mother's business, and though the physical assaults by the mother stopped when Rita entered her late teens, Rita was underpaid and overworked by her mother in the business and subject to frequent and public humiliations by her. These public shamings always occurred on the heels of a business reversal. Though the mother's drinking was usually the cause of these setbacks, the mother would find a way to blame Rita for them.

Rita engaged in numerous affairs with alcoholic men, who, like her mother, exploited her financially and emotionally and viciously assaulted her self-esteem. At the time she entered therapy, for example, she was heavily involved with a married man who was actively psychotic as well as actively alcoholic. Though he physically abused Rita when he was drinking, and required her constant attention and support in order to avoid complete fragmentation and institutionalization, Rita saw *him* as the victim. She felt that he was being abused by his estranged wife and she became completely absorbed in helping him to fight his wife on matters of custody and finance that naturally arose as a consequence of the couple's separation. When the wife triumphed in any of these conflicts, and on the frequent occasions when the estranged couple attempted to reconcile, Rita never faulted her lover for his masochism or inconstancy, but rather believed she had failed him in some substantial way. She felt completely worthless at such times.

Rita exhibited severe difficulty with the developmental task of separation and individuation. Her vocational activity and intimate associations were dictated by long-established familial patterns rather than personal values and native endowments.

Sam was another adult child whose history of failure and disappointment seemed to be the enactment of family destiny.

Sam

Sam was the 27-year-old son of an alcoholic mother. He was an extraordinarily bright and psychologically minded young man, and a promising artist. He came to therapy after being dismissed from a large state university where he was unable to finish any of the projects that were assigned in his art classes. He lived with his retired parents. Sam's mother, who had abandoned her own career as a commercial artist in order to marry and raise a family, censured Sam for his dependency on his family and was openly contemptuous of his artistic ambitions. Sam's father passively accepted the mother's assaults on Sam, as well as the attacks she mounted on his own self-worth.

Even though Sam was made miserable by his mother's criticisms and her drinking, and by the sadomasochistic relation between his parents, he never looked for well-paid work that would enable him to move away from home. In fact, he never even looked for a job that was appropriate to his interests and his considerable intellect, but worked as a busboy in a restaurant close to his parents' home. Despite his high intelligence and obvious talent, he felt incapable of any real academic, artistic, or vocational achievement. His romantic relationships tended to take the form of brief and disappointing affairs with alcoholic women, who proved to be unstable, unfaithful, and uninterested in real intimacy and commitment. Like Rita, he blamed the failure of his relationships on his own incompetence as a romantic partner.

Object relations theory offers a rationale for such failures to establish an adequately differentiated, cohesive identity or sense of self. Theorists believe that much of the self is formed through the alternate introjection, or incorporation, of people and parts of people who are outside the self, and the projection onto others of parts of the self that were previously introjected. Fairbairn, who spent a part of his career working with delinquent adolescents who had grown up in alcoholic homes, used the concept of introjection to explain the failure to separate from, and the development of intractable attachments to, difficult, disappointing, and destructive parents.

Fairbairn observed that since children are completely dependent on their parents for psychic and physical survival, they are in no position to reject and abandon destructive parents ([1943] 1981, 67). This dilemma is painfully prominent in the case histories that we take from adult children. Rita, for one, discovered early on that the tenderness she craved and the brutality she feared came in the same bewildering and terrifying package. One of her mother's frequent alcoholic rituals involved beating Rita with a piece of clothesline until the child's back was covered with bleeding welts and then confining her to her room. Sometime later, the mother would knock at the door of her daughter's room and issue an affectionate invitation to join her in baking a batch of cookies. Rita always accepted this invitation, and when she did, her mother would take her gently by the hand and lead her to the kitchen. It is critical to note that Rita did not lie in bed dreading her mother's return after these beatings, but rather, lay there praying for the knock on the door that signaled the possibility of rapprochment.

Fairbairn found that even in those situations in which children are physically abused, they refuse to see their parents as bad, but, instead accuse themselves of being bad children. He concluded that "bad relationships with objects" who are crucial to one's survival are psychically intolerable for children and that they cope by "taking the burden of badness' into themselves (p. 65). An abused and neglected child will deny the destructiveness of the parents, seize upon their destructive and disappointing qualities, and form from these a "bad object" that is then incorporated into her own psyche and becomes a part of the self. This has the agreeable effect of creating a secure, "good" outer field, but produces a hellish condition inside the child.

First, the child suffers a massive loss of self-esteem, since the self is experienced as possessing all the bad qualities of the object, such as rage, fragility and uncontrollability. As Fairbairn put it, the feeling of "outer security is . . . purchased at the price of inner security . . . [and the] ego is henceforth left at the mercy of a band of internal fifth columnists or persecutors" ([1943] 1981, 65).

Sam is another case in point here.

Despite high praise and vigorous encouragement from his art teachers, Sam believed himself to be an untalented and useless weakling. This self-perception was partially the result of his mother's projection of these qualities into him and it also represented an identification with her aggressive assault on a crucial aspect of his self. However, his lack of belief in himself was also the result of an active internalization of the failed artist that he beheld in his mother, and of the passive, retreating father who failed to protect Sam from his mother's rage.

Fairbairn remarked that the presence of these "bad objects" or inner "devils" in the psyche ultimately results in severe ego impoverishment, intense self-consciousness, and a deep subjective sense of futility and unreality. I believe that it is also responsible for the profound sense of hopelessness many adult children experience about the possibility of ever finding meaningful work or establishing stable and rewarding relationships. As Rita and Sam often said to me: "No normal person would ever want me, and I sure wouldn't know what to do with them."

Such words rise partly from a despair that is born of years of abnormal, destructive relatedness with parents and siblings; but they also express a conviction of inner damage and debasement that is the result of internalizing bad objects. Adult children often feel that they are so twisted, inadequate, and worthless that they are incapable of inspiring love and commitment from others. The feeling of impairment is deeper and more pervasive when there has been a great deal of frustration and abuse at the hands of one's parents. This is because so much more psychic territory and energy must then be give over to the containment of bad objects. For example, Rita, who was sexually abused and physically brutalized by her mother, had a nearly unshakable conviction of worthlessness which, at one time, fed her own dependency on psychoactive chemicals and which vastly increased the hopelessness she felt about the possibility of forming a relationship with a "normal" man or working successfully outside the family business.

Sam was emotionally harassed and exploited by his parents but never physically neglected or abused by either of them. His "devils" seemed fewer in number and less malignant than did Rita's. For example, while he had a deep fear that women, as well as prospective employers, would view him with the same critical eye that he habitually cast upon himself, this was, for Sam, a *fear*—not a conviction as it was with Rita—which probably helped him to avoid compulsive drinking and drugging. It certainly made it easier for him to sustain the modicum of hopefulness necessary to eventually proceed with separation and individuation by experimenting with new relationships and work roles. As time went on, he was even able to be productive with his art work, a sphere of activity that radically diverged from familial vocational traditions.

However, if an inner world populated by devils, saboteurs,

and persecutors is a world of hopelessness and despair, it is also a world of longing. Adult children long for love and they long for restoration. Fairbairn observed that it is the feeling that one's objects are basically good that confers a sense of security and essential goodness on the self. Kohut also said that reliable, empathic bonds with selfobjects are necessary for the development and maintenance of self-worth. So we may conjecture that the longing for restoration is, at its foundation, a longing for a good object that can provide a sustaining self–selfobject relation. As we have established, the introjection of bad objects leaves adult children with little faith in their ability to attract and hold good objects, so for them, the only feasible means of acquiring a good object and self–selfobject relation is to restore the damaged parent to a condition of wholeness and happiness. As Rita once explained to me, "If I am to feel good about myself, a phoenix *must* rise from the ashes."

Wurmser (1981) discovered a similar dynamic at work in those of his patients who seemed to find doomed relationships at every turn. They appeared to seek, in each new lover, the damaged and disappointing parent, and to relentlessly pursue his restoration. Wurmser found in this unconscious, compulsive process a "deeper reciprocity": The hidden belief of the individual that the restoration of the impaired loved one will also restore the damaged and suffering self (1981, 70). It may be somewhat more accurate to say that the adult child unconsciously seeks the restoration of the damaged parents, or parent surrogates, in order to secure an adequate self–selfobject relation that will strengthen the self and the sense of self-worth.

The restoration of a parent's troubled spirit and tortured psyche proves to be a formidable undertaking and one that is obviously incompatible with separation and individuation. On the contrary, it requires a tenacious, intense bond with the alcoholic and with all of those people encountered in life who come to represent the alcoholic in the adult child's unconscious mind. These bonds will be honored even when they pose enormous threats to the adult child's personal well-being. At one time, Rita would neglect classes at the university, stand up dates, cancel therapy appointments, and interrupt vacations in order to rescue either her mother or her current lover from various alcoholic pits into which they had fallen. During the particularly destructive affair with the man who was both psychotic and alcoholic, Rita felt compelled to withdraw from school and therapy altogether. It was obvious that the savings in psychic energy which she reaped as a result of these moves were fully invested in her campaign to prevent her lover's fragmentation. This campaign failed; the man was finally hospitalized and Rita relapsed.

The Attack on the Self: Narcissistic Vulnerability in Adult Children

Labile self-esteem seems almost endemic among children of alcoholics. While their demands on others can seem grandiose and arrogant at times, their self-estimation may fall dramatically in response to indications of imperfection in themselves or signs of disapproval from others. We have seen that the separation problems of adult children are overdetermined; it is likely that their narcissistic vulnerability derives from several sources as well.

Kohut's Self Psychology provides a framework for understanding many of the self-esteem problems that adult children experience. Alcoholic and alcohol-preoccupied parents are usually in a state of severe narcissistic imbalance themselves, and are therefore unable to provide the joyful and affirming acceptance that Kohut found essential for the development of secure self-esteem in the child. As Kohut might put it, the absence of adequate mirroring from selfobjects produces a deficit in self-esteem that is extremely difficult for adult children to overcome.

The previous section explained that self-esteem is also compromised by the child's effort to contain, within his own psyche, the disappointing and alarming aspects of the parents. The child's internalization of the parents' bad qualities has two roots. First, self-disgusted alcoholic parents and enabling spouses frequently project their self-disgust into their children. The children are too naïve, too loving, and too vulnerable to reject this pervasive gift. Rita's self-disgusted indictment of herself when her psychotic lover would fail or break down provides an illustration of the effects of projective identification on the self-esteem of an adult child. When Rita's lover was in trouble, he would attribute his incapacity or fragmentation to Rita's failure to offer him adequate physical or psychological support. These sorts of accusations constituted a familiar refrain for Rita, who was accustomed to being berated for business reverses that were actually the result of her mother's own alcohol-induced lapses. In both cases, Rita accepted the indictment and bitterly reviled herself for the negligence, disloyalty, and psychic disorganization that actually characterized her bad objects. This, of course, made her feel worthless.

Second, as the previous section also explained, the child actively seeks to control the parents' "bad" qualities by containing them within the self. This is a maneuver which drastically depresses self-esteem since it alters the very structure of the self to include the "bad object structures" that contain contemptible aspects of the parent. This phenomenon is clearly seen in both Rita and Sam. For Fairbairn, it explained why, when "the child's objects present themselves to him as bad, he himself feels "bad" ([1943] 1981, 64).

In addition to making the individual feel "bad," however, bad object structures in the psyche claim a portion of the ego for their own, and thereby become capable of vicious attacks upon other parts of the ego and the self. Fairbairn called the portion of the ego that exists in principal relation to the bad object structures the antilibidinal ego. He also referred to it as the "internal saboteur," since it has such a deleterious effect on the personality and behavior. He believed that the fundamental pain his patients experienced involved their extreme libidinal frustration at the hands of their parents, who tended to be abusive and neglectful in the extreme. He observed that the internal saboteur embodies the frustrating, rejecting, abusive qualities of the parents and is identified with their aggressive attitude toward the child's dependency needs. He noted further that the internal saboteur, which is split off from the central ego and is therefore an unconscious entity, also contains, and is strengthened by, the child's own feelings of aggression toward the hurtful, depriving parents—aggression which cannot be safely directed at the parent, and is therefore repressed. The saboteur directs "a maximum" (Fairbairn [1944] 1981, 114–115) of its aggression against the parts of the self that experience a longing for objects and strive for connections to them (the internalized exciting objects and the libidinal ego). This causes the longing (of the libidinal ego, or Guntrip's lost heart of the self) to be split off from consciousness with other frightened aspects of the "true" self.

Paul was an adult child who suffered frequent and devastating attacks from an internal saboteur. As a very young child, he was usually left in the daily care of his severely depressed and drug-dependent father, since his mother supported the family. Paul's father was so depressed that he spent most days lying in bed, or vacantly staring at the television screen. He provided Paul with the minimal care necessary, but rarely attempted to play with him or provide him with any other form of psychological sustenance. He left Paul to search within himself for necessary emotional gratification, and like many of Kohut's chronically understimulated patients, Paul at first became a compulsive masturbator, and later, a compulsive overeater and pornography addict.

Paul actually recognized that masturbation, food, and pornography provided him with physical pleasures that were a disappointing substitute for the emotional relatedness he craved, but he found himself unable to reach for such relatedness. Whenever Paul looked at another human being with longing, an inner voice (the saboteur) caustically denounced his feelings as "babyish" and exhorted him to "stand on his own two feet like a man." This voice also warned him that any overt expression of his intense longing to another person would certainly cause that person to retreat in disgust. These shrieks of disapproval from the internal saboteur made Paul ashamed of his normal narcissistic needs for a sustaining self–selfobject relation and caused him to split off his longing and bury it along with other aspects of his true self. Thus psychically numbed, he would proceed to withdraw from the potentially intimate situation that had triggered his longing. This withdrawal, and the wave of emptiness which followed in its wake, inevitably provoked a depressive episode of the sort Paul had witnessed in his father, with Paul taking to bed, collapsing in front of the T.V., or indulging his own compulsion of choice, pornographic movies.

At one point, a grown-up Paul asked his father, who had recovered from his depression and maintained a stable sobriety for some years, to help him pay for psychotherapy. Interestingly, the father attacked the idea of therapy, and observed that if Paul were really a man, he would "stand on his own two feet." Clearly, the internal saboteur had adopted the father's own strategy for handling Paul's dependency needs. Though the saboteur hampered Paul in his struggle to achieve rewarding connectedness with others, it probably had served an adaptive function at one time, in sparing Paul this sort of rejection from his father. It is my experience that the internal saboteur will attack not only the child's dependency needs, but any quality of the child's self that originally threatened the parent and caused her to attack the child. For example, Sam's internal saboteur constantly assaulted his individuation needs and thwarted his efforts to separate, just as his mother did.

When the true self reaches out to its selfobjects for intimacy and support and is furiously assaulted by the internal saboteur for its trouble, this crushes the self-esteem of the adult child, who comes to view normal dependency and narcissistic needs as infantile and shameful. However, it also provokes a sudden withdrawal from the object(s), and, as Guntrip observed, this sort of behavior lends an "in and out" quality to relationships (1969, 36). Therefore, this discussion of the internal saboteur will be expanded in the following section, which discusses the instability of the adult child.

The Instability of the Adult Child

The social, romantic, and vocational commitments of adult children are frequently erratic and extreme. This behavioral instability appears to spring from a psychic instability produced by the internalization of unstable "bad" objects and by pervasive splitting of the personality.

Psychic Splitting and Fear of Dependency and Attachment in the Adult Child

Adult children long for love and intimacy, but are terrified of the high price that may be exacted should they open themselves to the possibility of deep connectedness to others. They are understandably afraid that the attachments of adult life will hurt them as badly as did the family relationships they knew as children. They fear that each new involvement will result in further exploitation, abuse, and betrayal. However, the attachment–withdrawal dilemma may also be understood at a deeper level. It is the very dilemma that Fairbairn and Guntrip termed the "schizoid problem."

Once again, the occurrence of a true-self-false-self split in adult children occurs on account of an inability in alcoholic and alcohol-preoccupied parents to adapt to or tolerate certain qualities in the child. In many alcoholic homes, children's naturally extreme dependency is especially intolerable to the parents, who feel overwhelmed by their own problems, and underprepared for parenthood. Like Paul's father, and the parents of Jack and Ed, these parents are neglectful in the face of their children's needs and, at times, even punish the expression of normal needs.

Fairbairn and Guntrip explained that when children come to regard their own dependency needs as bad and shameful and begin to believe that their longing for love and support, made desperately intense by chronic emotional deprivation, alienates and even destroys those they long for, they try to annihilate such feelings at all costs. This is the goal of the internal saboteur. Like Paul, Jack, and Ed, these individuals split off their longing for others and thus, emotionally numbed, tell themselves they have no reason to enter into close relationships. Some of these withdrawals into self are accomplished with an attitude of arrogance, and others in a state of utter hopelessness; but the result is the same: unstable relationships and extreme social and emotional isolation.

Split-off dependency needs and narcissistic longings do emerge in the consciousness of adult children from time to time, but rarely make themselves felt in the presence of potentially nurturant others. They are more prone to emerge in the presence of other people who have deep attachment fears. This was certainly the case with Ed, who could feel tenderness and longing only for women who were compulsive abandoners. One extended involvement with an alcoholic woman was the model for all of Ed's relationships with women. These two would be inseparable for a period, making plans for an idyllic future together. Inevitably, however, the woman would go on a drinking binge and betray Ed with another man. Ed would banish her from his life, and, not infrequently, he would also get drunk himself, and beat her up before throwing her out. After a brief separation, however, one or the other would beg for forgiveness, the couple would reconcile, and the whole cycle would begin in motion once again.

Ed's irresistible attraction to such women was based partly

on a wish to rehabilitate bad objects (his mother, stepmother, and father, all of whom had hurt or abandoned him in some significant way), but it was also designed to avoid a real attachment, which would have had an infinite capacity to inflict pain on him by making possible a much deeper loss—of the sort he had experienced with his mother. Though Ed seldom questioned his attraction to abandoners, he was deeply suspicious of tender feelings toward others and longings for connectedness to them, and he became frightened when these feelings began to emerge in more appropriate contexts. On one occasion, he stopped to watch a father playing hide and seek with his young son in the park, and felt himself deeply moved by the exuberant display of affection between the man and the boy, who concluded each episode of the game with a bear hug and a kiss. Ed was stunned to find himself tearful over this scene, describing his reaction as "bizarre, totally bizarre." He related it to the quality of wimpiness that his father so often noticed in him. In truth, his response represented the initial healing of the split between central ego and libidinal ego and the burgeoning of a healthy ability to tolerate, in consciousness, normal longing for connectedness to another human being (or, in Kohutian terms, the normal longing for the sustaining responsiveness of a reliably empathic selfobject). It was an encouraging reentry into the world of enhancing, as opposed to destructive, human relationships.

The Return of the Bad Object

The splitting off of normal longings for relationships with empathically responsive others makes the establishment of stable commitments and relationships impossible. However, there is another psychic situation that promotes instability in adult children of alcoholics. Fairbairn observed that repressed bad objects may be traumatically "released" when conditions in outer reality come to closely resemble an unconscious paradigm ([1943] 1981, 76–78). He specifically referred to the way that abusive conditions of armed combat seem to trigger memories of parental abuse in some soldiers. In Fairbairn's experience such memories frequently stimulated violent imagery, with the soldiers picturing themselves as victims of abuse, or as being abusive to others. Fairbairn remarked that in these cases the repressed bad objects had "returned with a vengeance" ([1943] 1981, 77). Fairbairn regarded these situations as transference phenomena, since external conditions had acquired the significance of repressed ones involving relationships with bad objects. It is crucial to understand, however, that it is an *unsatisfactory object relationship* that has been repressed, not merely a "bad" feeling, such as anger or lust. Accordingly, what emerges in response to a traumatic stimulus is not just a feeling, but a repressed part of the self structure—the internalized bad object and one's relation to it. Certain aspects of the adult child's instability, such as the chameleon-like, Jekyll and Hyde transformations in behavior that were described in chapter 2, can be explained by applying Fairbairn's notions about the traumatic return of repressed bad objects.

Chapter 2 explained that the long-suffering, self-sacrificing individual who wears the hero's mantle by day, may display the scapegoat's colors on other occasions, giving little doubt as to an underlying capacity for rebellion and aggression. Another clear example of this sort of psychic split was provided by Tom, a police detective who was the adult child of an alcoholic mother. Tom's most cherished roles at work emphasized protection and rescue, and he spent much of the little free time available to him working to find jobs and meaningful community service activities for troubled adolescents whom he met in the course of performing volunteer work for a religious organization. This individual, a genuinely dedicated and compassionate young man, was the subject of numerous brutality complaints, not only from persons he arrested, but also from uninvolved witnesses to these arrests. Tom never denied these charges, but saw his behavior as justified in each case, and felt it presented no contradiction to other aspects of his life.

Like many other adult children, Tom was caught in the infinite loop of familial alcoholism. While he himself was sober, he had created a lifestyle that brought him into constant contact with people who were as traumatically disappointing and disillusioning to him as the mother who alternately beat him and abandoned him. (The population he served included a large number of drug-involved individuals.) Because Tom was workaholic, and carried his redemptive crusade into his so-called "leisure" time, his exposure to traumatic disappointment was nearly unrelieved. His relentless effort to restore the bad objects of the world did indeed constitute a sort of combat situation for Tom. He had re-created the war zone of his childhood, where he had been the solitary, heroic guardian of peace and virtue.

This position, chronically and doggedly maintained throughout his childhood and young adulthood, severely depleted and fatigued Tom's psychological defenses. When he was then confronted with some sudden traumatic disappointment that was similar to those he had experienced as a child, these defenses were quickly overwhelmed. The break-up of an affair or a severe dressing down by a superior were two situations that proved especially devastating to Tom, perhaps because he had felt both betrayed and abused by his mother. When Tom's defenses broke down, the repressed, abusive, bad object relationships of *his* childhood returned with a vengeance. That is, the effort to contain the bad object relationships in his own psyche, so that the outside world felt somewhat secure, no longer worked. Instead, the outside world once again felt like a hopeless, destructive place, and Tom, who was ordinarily the cheerful backslapping embodiment of a "hale fellow well met," found himself fighting waves of black despair and crying quietly to himself as he pursued such mundane tasks as painting his mother's house.

With his inner devils once again loose in the world, Tom felt like the frightened and desperate little boy he had once been. Like Ed, he coped with these intolerable feelings of vulnerability by reactively identifying with the aggressor—becoming, for a period, his abusive mother and beating unmercilessly those who were helpless before him. This is, perhaps, another aspect of the "return" of the bad object: Pervasive splitting of the personality creates a psychic situation that is inherently unstable, and the part of the self that is identified with the rejecting, abusive parent (the antilibidinal ego) may, under traumatic conditions such as those outlined by Fairbairn, assume a position of primacy in the psyche, temporarily displacing the central ego as the governor of behavior. This provides an explanation of the extreme and frightening shifts of role, behavior, mood, and perspective that are so often seen in adult children of alcoholics.

Summary

Children of alcoholics tend to encounter many serious problems as they attempt to fulfill the demands of adult life: They often have great difficulty separating and individuating from their families; they are liable to have trouble maintaining adequate and stable levels of self-esteem; and they are frequently unable to make steadfast commitments in work or love. Perhaps most importantly, children of alcoholics seem drawn to an alcoholic lifestyle, and are likely to become deeply and painfully involved with partners, causes, and compulsions that endanger their physical, psychological, and spiritual well-being. The source of these problems is a disturbance of the parent–child relationship in alcoholic homes. Instead of providing their children with support, encouragement, and unconditional regard, alcoholic and enabling spouses are likely to abuse, exploit, and neglect them. When children are hurt by their selfobjects instead of nurtured by them, the result is a severe disturbance of the internal object relationships that form the foundation of the self and extensive fragmentation (splitting) of the psyche that also weakens the self.

First the "true," or nuclear, self—when it feels itself threatened by the parents—retreats to a place of hiding in the unconscious. That is, it is "split off" from the central, conscious ego. Though the true self may make its existence known through acts of impulse or subjectively experienced longing, it is never allowed direct expression and remains alienated from, and misunderstood by, the conscious self. A "false self" arises to carry on conscious transactions with the external world and to provide the true self with the camouflage it feels it needs. Though the false self may contain many socially valued elements, and may realize a certain degree of success in academic and vocational pursuits, it is inherently unstable, and never feels entirely "real" to the adult child. Moreover, feelings of frustration, futility, and loneliness emanate from the true self, isolated as it is, and deprived of meaningful intrapsychic and interpersonal intercourse. These feelings periodically build up, overwhelm the adult child's capacity to split and repress, and become outright, conscious psychic pain. The erection of a false self also interferes with the struggle to separate and individuate, since it masks and weakens the parts of the self that are truly distinctive and that form the "lost heart of the self" necessary for the full realization of one's individuality.

The self of the adult child is also damaged by the individual's effort to psychically contain "bad" (abusive, exploitative, neglectful) aspects of the parent. The internalization of bad objects represents, in part, a passive acceptance of parental projections and relatively passive processes of identification with dramatic aspects of parental character. However, it is also the result of the child's active effort to secure a portion of the external environment by taking its more frightening aspects into the self. This is a strategy which severely depletes self-esteem, promotes a sense of hopelessness in the adult child, and requires further harmful splitting of the psyche. It also leads to a futile attempt to restore the self by rehabilitating bad objects. This creates the "infinite loop" of familial alcoholism—an endless cycle of disappointment and despair.

Internalized bad objects become a part of the (unconscious) ego and become capable of attacking other parts of the ego and the self. The part of the ego most at risk is that which recognizes a need for empathic connectedness to other people—for psychologically sustaining selfobject relationships. This "libidinal ego," as Fairbairn would call it, is particularly vulnerable because it is so often attacked by alcoholic and enabling parents, who are relatively unable to provide an adequate selfobject environment for their children. When the antilibidinal ego of the adult child, identified with the rejecting aspect of the parents, attacks the libidnal ego, this further damages self-esteem. It also causes a withdrawal from potentially intimate, satisfying selfobject relationships, making the adult child appear and feel unstable, and leaving him more isolated and lonely as well.

Though bad objects, and the parts of the self that are identified with them are normally repressed or split off from consciousness, they may be released by a traumatic incident. The alcoholic lifestyle in which many adult children are immersed subjects them to chronic stress and frequent traumatic disappointments that evoke the pains of the childhood home and cause repressed memories and bad object relationships to penetrate to consciousness. When adult children feel trapped, once again, in a dangerous, sadomasochistic world, they may reactively identify with the perceived aggressor and become abusive, exploitative, and/or neglectful themselves. This is another aspect of instability in adult children.

It should be fairly obvious that the defects of self to which adult children are frequently heir operate in a circular fashion to ensure an unending series of painful defeats. For example, unstable self-esteem creates an unwillingness in adult children to enter into new activities or relationships that could strengthen the self and the feelings of self-worth. The failure to form new, more healthful attachments further hampers adult children's efforts to separate from unsatisfying, hurtful relationships with family members. When adult children are not able to separate from their destructive parents and siblings, this further damages their self-esteem. The unrelieved exposure to destructive relationships deepens their hopelessness about the entire object world. This hopelessness reinforces the need to submerge the true self, and promotes unstable relationships and psychological isolation. This leads to more problems with self-esteem, and so forth. A psychotherapy that serves to reveal and strengthen the true self can therapeutically pierce this vicious circle of failure and continued damage to the self.

5

THE RESTORATION
OF PSYCHIC STRUCTURE
IN PSYCHOTHERAPY

THE BRITISH object relations theorists, and Heinz Kohut, proposed models of psychotherapy that aim to uncover, clarify, and strengthen key aspects of psychic structure that have been distorted or badly damaged in struggles with parents. These theorists have all suggested that certain critical aspects of the true self have been driven into hiding (repressed or split off) as a means to preserve them. They thus believed that psychotherapy should aim at the liberation of the hidden self, and its integration into the central sector of the psyche. Their approaches to the unification of the psyche, or as Kohut would have it the restoration of the self, are remarkably similar in many respects and diverge dramatically from the classical approach to resolution of transference neuroses. Perhaps the structural approach is most easily understood by comparing it to psychoanalytic perspectives on several important aspects of treatment, including therapeutic goals, the nature of transference, the problem of defense and resistance, and the process and technique of psychotherapy.

The Goals of Treatment

The classical approach to analysis and analytically informed psychotherapy emphasizes the analysis of repressed sexual and aggressive impulses and their integration into conscious life. Liberating libidinal energy by lifting extensive repression allows the patient to seek and obtain gratification in work and love. Freud believed that self-regard was gained mainly through gratification of object libido (having love returned and possessing the loved object) and the sufficiently successful pursuit of the ego-ideal, which he conceived as a model ego, based on identifications with parents or with collective ideals (LaPlanche and Pontalis 1973, 44). When analysis is successful, the patient gives up the possibility of actual gratification of instinctual urges that are at odds with the demands of civilized adult life. He also accepts gratifications which can be realized in relationships with nonincestuous love objects as well as through sublimation of instinctual urges in the pursuit of culturally approved ideals.

Object relations theory—as it was conceived by the British school—and Kohut's Self Psychology, aim at much different goals. They are concerned with the analysis of early environmental failure, its devastating impact on the evolution of psychic structure, and bringing to consciousness those structural elements that have been repressed or split off from consciousness as a result of environmental trauma. Like psychoanalysis, these two theories aim at a loosening of ties to infantile objects, but they are not centrally concerned with the maturation and sublimation of sexual instinct. They seek instead the release from the unconscious of the massively destructive objects that the patient has internalized in the course of "bad" relationships with parents, and the subsequent renewal of the patient's self, and self-regard, in relationships with supportive and loving objects.

Winnicott believed that a child's true self is driven into hiding by the parents' failure to adapt to compelling psychic and physical needs that the child experiences in early life. He found that the splitting off of the true self leads to psychic instability as well as great subjective distress. Winnicott proposed that the analytic situation provides an opportunity for an analyst to facilitate the emergence of the true self. He felt that under conditions of considerable psychological safety the false self can be surrendered, and the true self can penetrate to consciousness. The psychic split finally healed, the patient recovers her individuality and vitality and discovers a "new sense of self" ([1954a] 1975, 290).

Fairbairn was also concerned with the reunion of a pervasively split psyche. Like Winnicott, he felt that psychic splits are the result of parental failure, especially extremes of neglect and abuse. Where Winnicott saw a true-self–false-self split, however Fairbairn saw a "multiplicity of repressed egos" ([1944] 1981, 94), each associated with "bad" (neglectful or abusive) aspects of the parent(s). He thought that the goal of psychotherapy should be to alter the "basic endopsychic situation" (p. 109), which consists of pitched and painful warfare between these psychic structures as they vie for control of the individual's pursuit of objects. In Fairbairn's scheme, it will be remembered, the central ego attacks both the antilibidinal and libidinal egos, as well as their objects, and the antilibidinal ego attacks the libidinal ego and its object. While Fairbairn said that one of the most important aims of psychoanalytic therapy is a reduction in the split of the original ego, he felt that this lofty goal can never be fully achieved, and that the analyst should also aim at amelioration of psychic distress in other ways. He charged analysts with the task of dissolving the bonds between the subsidiary egos and their respective objects, and reducing the aggression of the antilibidinal ego (the internal saboteur) toward the libidinal ego and its object.

Harry Guntrip's view of the fundamental problem for analysis is quite close to the views of Winnicott and Fairbairn. He believed that the psychic fault separating "the utilitarian self of everyday conscious living and the fear-ridden infantile ego in a state of schizoid withdrawnness" (1969, 299) must somehow be filled and sealed. He also felt that, in those cases in which "radical" psychotherapy, aimed at regrowing the "whole personal self," is an economically, intellectually, and psychologically fea-

sible aim for the patient and therapist, it should strive for something more than the resolution of particular conflicts in the
individual's life. The ultimate goal, for Guntrip, was the "regrowing of the basic ego, the whole personal self" (1969, 317).

Kohut described the "essential task of psychotherapy" in
much the same terms as the British theorists did. He said that
a good analysis must explore the flaws in the structure of the self,
strengthen "the existing fabric of the self," and lay down new
self structures to "fill the defects of self" that hinder the patient
(1984, 99–100) These efforts, Kohut believed, enable the patient
to fulfill the program of the nuclear self in matters of love and
work. Kohut also said that successful analysis results in a fundamental change in the nature of the patient's relationship to
selfobjects. The patient whose self becomes harmonious and secure in analysis will no longer seek desperately after the response
of archaic selfobjects. On the contrary, the restored self will be
satisfied and sustained by the "empathic resonance" of the
selfobjects of adult life (1984, 70). Kohut believed, in fact, that
the "essence of cure" resides in the patient's increased ability
to "identify and seek out appropriate selfobjects—both mirroring and idealizable—...and to be sustained by them" (1984,
77).

Defense and Resistance

The classical conception of defense involves the idea that the
ego must defend the individual against threats to well-being that
stem from unconscious aggressive and sexual urges. As these
urges press for satisfaction in reality, the ego employs a number
of strategies designed to maintain them, and the painful affects
that are associated with them, in the relative safety of the unconscious. Freud employed the term "resistance" to refer to any
defensive effort by a patient to prevent the analyst from exposing
the patient's unconscious desires. When Rita told me of being

humiliated or beaten by her mother, I always asked her to search for and describe the feelings she experienced during and after the incident. She found it nearly impossible to do so, and always told me, "The feelings flash by. I can't hold on to them long enough to tell you about them." A classical interpretation of Rita's resistance to sharing her emotional experience with me would likely emphasize her reluctance to confront her rage toward her mother. The following material will explain why a structural theorist would be more likely to link Rita's blocking emotion in the session to her unconscious effort to restrain the longing of her battered, dependent, and deeply hidden true self to share its hurt with me and to experience me as a soothing, maternal selfobject.

The British theorists departed from classical analytic theory to advance the idea that, in some cases, psychopathology can be traced to structural anomalies in the psyche. Their conception of a massively split psyche and an embattled self driven underground required them to elucidate the strategies that the self might employ in its struggle to survive. Their efforts greatly expanded classical notions concerning defense and resistance, and pointed toward a revolutionary declaration by Kohut in 1984 that "the so-called defense-resistances are neither defenses nor resistances" but rather, "valuable moves to safeguard the self." (1984, 141). The adult child has typically mastered a variety of strategies designed to conceal and protect a severely damaged core self from further injury. He is on guard against anyone, including a psychotherapist, who may reveal this core and expose it to more harm. Psychotherapists must understand the real meaning of these strategies in order to respond to them effectively.

Winnicott conceived of a "central or true self" that contains the "inherited potential" of the individual and which, under normal circumstances, acquires "at its own speed a personal psychic reality" (1975, xxxviii). He proposed that any threat to this normal course of development of the true self engenders profound anxiety, and even in early infancy promotes the erection of psychological defenses to ward off the "impingements" that threaten the self.

Winnicott saw the repression of the true self and the adoption and elaboration of the false self as the principal defense of the individual against severe failures of parental adaptation. He said that the false self serves to "freeze the failure situation" and emphasized that it is "normal and healthy" for the person to defend the self in this way ([1954a] 1975, 281). He also said that this defensive strategy reflects a hope that the psychological dilemma the individual faces may eventually find a happy resolution:

> Along with this [freezing of the failure situation] goes an unconscious assumption (which can become a conscious hope) that opportunity will occur at a later date for a renewed experience in which the failure situation will be able to be unfrozen and re-experienced, with the individual in a regressed state, in an environment that is making adequate adaptation. ([1954a] 1975, 281).

Winnicott's ideas about a healing "regression to dependence" in an adequately adapted psychotherapeutic environment are discussed below.

Fairbairn openly challenged Freud's idea that it is only libido that is repressed in the event of psychic conflict. He viewed instinct as "inseparable from (psychic) structure," as "representing simply the dynamic aspect of structure" ([1944] 1981, 119) and, like Winnicott, saw the repression of psychic structure as a centrally important defensive maneuver.

Fairbairn, once again, believed that a variety of psychic structures are repressed in response to environmental trauma. He called the repression of the exciting and rejecting objects by the undivided central ego "direct repression" ([1944] 1981, 115). In his view, the ego secondarily rejects two parts of itself that are attached to the two internal objects (the libidinal ego and the antilibidinal ego, or internal saboteur, respectively) and re-

presses them. The repression of the objects and their corresponding subsidiary egos constitutes "direct repression" (p. 115) in
Fairbairn's parlance. He called the aggression of the internal
saboteur against the libidinal ego and the exciting object "in-
direct repression" (p. 118) since it is a "very powerful factor in
furthering" the direct repression of the structures that offend
the central ego (p. 116).

Fairbairn found that the attachment of the libidinal ego to the
exciting object, while itself a result of direct repression, also
serves to maintain repression and to divert the individual away
from outer reality. He said that it therefore "constitutes a particularly formidable source of resistance—and one which plays
no small part in determining what is known as the negative
therapeutic reaction" ([1944] 1981, 117). This is to say, the patient abandons the internalized bad objects with extreme reluctance and defends mightily against their release from the
unconscious. This is because the objects were initially internalized in a sort of "pact with Satan" ([1943] 1981, 70) that the
patient entered in a desperate effort to establish control over
their intolerable badness. The patient fears to surrender the
repressed objects lest the environment once again become "peo-
pled with devils which are too terrifying for him to face" (p. 69).
Fairbairn described the frightening quandary that the patient
faces upon entering psychotherapy:

> It is true that it is from his symptoms that [the patient] con-
> sciously desires to be relieved, and that a considerable proportion
> of psychopathological symptoms consist essentially in defences
> against a "return of the repressed" (i.e. a return of repressed
> objects). Nevertheless, it is usually when his defences are wearing
> thin and are proving inadequate to safeguard him against anxiety
> over a threatened release of repressed objects that he is driven to
> seek analytical aid. From the patient's point of view, accordingly,
> the effect of analytical treatment is to promote the very situation
> from which he seeks to escape. . . . he is not slow to realize that
> he is being cured by means of a hair from the tail of the dog that
> bit him. ([1943] 1981, 75)

Fairbairn believed that the patient's guilt about being bad represents an effort to maintain the repression of the bad objects, and should be regarded as a resistance to psychotherapy and to the analyst's efforts to release and expose the objects that have been buried in the unconscious.

Guntrip felt that the principal effect of parental abuse and neglect is to menace the very "selfhood" of a child and that defenses are raised in the interest of protecting the independence and freedom of determination of the self (1969, 289). He agreed with Winnicott and Fairbairn that the fundamental defensive strategy that the individual employs is to split off the needy and fearful part of the self, and he emphasized that the individual seeks thereby to withdraw the "heart of the self" from potentially harmful interactions with other people.

Guntrip thought that his schizoid patients had been taught from childhood to despise dependence on other people and that they greatly feared the weakness and need of the hidden self, which he also called the "regressed ego" (1969, 74) and which he viewed as the "headquarters of all the most serious fears" (p. 307). Guntrip found that his patients went to enormous lengths to avoid needing and interacting with others, since they feared that the exposure of their needs would throw them back on "the weakest part of [the] self." He said that the "ultimate meaning" of Fairbairn's antilibidinal ego is that "it enshrines the frightened child's fear of his own weakness, his desperate struggle to overcome it by self-forcing methods and by the denial of all needs....a struggle based on identification with rejective persons in real life" (p. 284). He found that this identification with rejecting parents (the libidinal cathexis of the bad object) formed the basis for a resistance to a good relationship with the analyst and the exposure of the regressed ego. Guntrip, much as Winnicott and Fairbairn, felt that this exposure, this "controlled constructive regression," represents the only path to recovery and regrowth (p. 284).

Though Guntrip's patients were terrified of further damage to the heart of the self, they also proved to be terrified of the profound aloneness that their withdrawal from other people engendered. They therefore attempted to walk a narrow line between their twin terrors, engaging in just enough relatedness with others to stave off profound loneliness, and staying sufficiently detached from others to avoid the possibility of further harm to the self. Guntrip called this strategy the "schizoid compromise" and said that its fundamental purpose is to retain relationships in a form that does not require a complete emotional engagement. (1969, 58–66) He said that schizoid patients employ this strategy in all relationships, and that it is actually rather easy to accomplish such a compromise in the analytic relationship.

Guntrip believed that schizoid patients are always resisting, to some extent, real dependence on the therapist, and that they have a variety of means at their disposal to do so. He described the "blocked analysis" as one of the most common forms of the schizoid compromise. In this case, the patient keeps coming to sessions, but never presents any real emotional issues for analysis: "He dare not give up, or serious anxiety will break out, and he dare not 'let go' and take the plunge into genuine analysis, or just as serious anxiety will be released." (1969, 294) He found that another compromise technique commonly practiced by these patients is to turn analysis into an intellectual discussion "about religion, or morality, or human relations in society, or their doubts about psychoanalysis" (p. 297). Other patients may compromise by establishing "half-in-and-half-out relationships" in "real life" and hiding these from the analyst. Guntrip said that such patients never "properly 'belong' to anything." Their nature is that of "a dilettante smatterer, toying with life rather than living it . . . like a butterfly alighting for a time then flitting on" (p. 302). Guntrip offered drug dependency as one example of this sort of compromise.

Finally, Guntrip felt that classical analysis itself might be used by some schizoid patients as a way to mark time without ever

really confronting the needs of the hidden self (1969, 303). He
warned that if analysts encourage their patients to regard sex
and aggression as the ultimate bases of the their conflicts, their
patients will never discover that these issues are only defenses
against the more fundamental fears of intimacy and aloneness.
Guntrip remarked in this connection that sexual relationships
in reality and fantasy are frequently a defensive substitute for
real relationships with real people (p. 306).

Guntrip remarked that the schizoid patient is "bound to be
on the defensive against the very person whose help he seeks"
and that all through treatment, such individuals will be "tossed
about between...fears of isolations and...fears of emotional
proximity (1969, 289). He asserted that the schizoid compromise
inevitably presents itself "in a thousand forms" throughout
treatment as the patient struggles with the issues of ' "near and
far,' dependence and independence, trust and distrust, acceptance of and resistance to treatment, the need of a security-giving
relationship and fear of all relationships as a threat to one's
separate existence" (p. 292). He thought that it is critical for the
therapist to understand that this kind of oscillation does not
reflect mere "perverseness, or negative transference, or moral
fault," but that it is a perfectly understandable effort by a self
that has been mortally threatened to defend its very existence
(p. 296).

It fell to Heinz Kohut to completely overthrow the classical
model of defense and resistance. While Kohut found the classical
view helpful in understanding transference neurosis, he called
it "unsatisfactory...in explaining personality in general and the
psychopathology of personality disturbances in particular—especially disturbances in which the essential psychopathology
results from the "thwarted development of the self" (1984, 113).
Kohut said that he preferred to speak of the "defensiveness" of
patients, rather than their "resistance" to treatment. He clearly
felt that any effort by a patient to hide the self from the therapist
is undertaken in the interest of preserving the self against "de-

struction and invasion" and "takeover" and that this is the patient's only purpose in "resisting" or thwarting the therapist:

> Defense motivation in analysis will be understood in terms of activities undertaken in the service of psychological survival, that is, as the patient's attempt to save at least that sector of his nuclear self, however small and precariously established it may be, that he has been able to construct and maintain despite serious insufficiencies in the development-enhancing matrix of the selfobjects of childhood. (1984, 115)

Kohut viewed the existence of defensive structures in the psyche as an example of the operation of the "principle of the primacy of self-preservation" (1984, 143). Like Winnicott, he saw defensive activity as an indication of the individual's undying hope for future recovery and continued self-development. He believed that if therapists can understand this deeper meaning of psychological defense, then the further growth of the nuclear self is indeed possible.

The Nature of Transference

Freud greatly enlarged our understanding of the complex psychic interplay between patient and psychotherapist with his concept of transference. He believed that transferential phenomena are at the heart of all human relationships, and that cure in psychoanalysis depends on an accurate understanding and interpretation of their operation in the analytic relationship.

Freud believed that "expectant libidinal impulses" are inevitably aroused in an individual whose need for love is substantially ungratified, by "each new person coming upon the scene." Therefore, he found it natural that unconscious, unsatisfied libidinal wishes are turned toward the analyst; that "the figure of the physician [is weaved] into one of the 'series' already constructed in [the patient's] mind" (Freud [1912] 1959, 313). Freud saw transference phenomena as an invaluable source of information about the patient, since the content of the wishes expressed toward the analyst plainly reveal the nature of the conflicts which are hindering the individual's effort to work and love. However, he also saw the transference as the most powerful weapon at the patient's disposal for *resistance* to the cure. The analytic cure, of course, rests on the exposure of repressed sexual and aggressive wishes, and Freud discovered that transference issues (in particular, negative feelings toward the analyst) seem to become prominent just at those moments in the analysis when significant repressed material appears likely to penetrate the patient's consciousness, and that they serve to effectively block the flow of associations. Freud conceived of a battle between patient and analyst, "a struggle . . . between intellect and the forces of instinct, between recognition and the striving for discharge" that is "fought out almost entirely over the transference-manifestations" (p. 322).

The British theorists and Kohut also saw the analyst's accurate understanding and careful handling of transference phenomena as the principal instrument of cure in psychoanalytic psychotherapy. In their work, however, the concept was gradually enlarged so that it has now come to include the idea that repressed or split-off aspects of the self, including affects, unfulfilled needs, and the object relationships that are associated with them, inevitably reemerge in the context of the therapy relationship. Furthermore, these theorists viewed the defensive aspects of transference as adaptive efforts to protect the wounded self from further damage. They did not view analysis of transference as a struggle between the patient and the analyst, but conceived of the analyst as struggling to understand the painful condition of a divided, distorted, and hidden self, and to communicate this understanding to the patient.

Winnicott obviously believed that something deeper than a transference, or displacement, of affects and needs from one object onto another occurs in psychotherapy. He tried to convey the largeness and complexity of the transference experience in cases of pronounced true-self–false-self splitting by saying that, "Whereas in the transference neurosis the past comes into the consulting-room, in this work it is more true to say that the present goes back into the past, and *is* the past.... the analyst finds himself confronted with the patient's primary process in the setting in which it had its original validity." ([1955] 1975, 297–298) He expanded upon this idea by saying, "one digs down to solid rock, by which I mean that one sees real things re-lived in this work" ([1948] 1975, 167).

Winnicott explained that, under conditions of "good enough adaptation" by the analyst, the patient's ego can begin to "re-call" the parents' original failures, which heretofore have been kept out of consciousness, and to become angry about them. These experiences of recall are first manifest in the patient's capacity to respond angrily to some failure on the part of the analyst, as if it were an original parental failure. He said, "Fail-ures there must be and indeed there is no attempt to give perfect adaptation.... The clue is that the analyst's failure is being used and must be treated as a *past* failure, one that the patient can perceive and encompass, and be angry about now." ([1955] 1975, 298) Winnicott said that patients "use" the analyst's errors to become angry, for the first time, about parental failures that were supremely disruptive when they occurred. He saw this development as a key occurrence in the therapy, and thought that analysts' responses to this type of patient anger largely determine the ultimate success or failure of treatment.

Winnicott found that many of his patients seemed to briefly withdraw from waking reality during their sessions with him, in some cases, actually dozing off. Winnicott saw these episodes as transferential—that his patients were reliving an early con-dition of need and incapacity. Further, they were coping with their reawakened needs by doing what they had likely been called upon to do as children. That is, instead of looking to the analyst for care and support, they were withdrawing and, in effect, "holding" themselves. Winnicott felt that if the analyst can manage to "hold" the patient by deeply understanding what the patient is experiencing during these momentary withdrawals, the withdrawal can be turned into a constructive "regression to dependence" in which the patient learns to trust that he may safely reveal the neediness and longing of the true self to another. ([1954a] 1975, 290–291)

Fairbairn emphasized the "psychopathological return of bad objects" as an important transference phenomenon ([1943] 1981, 75–76). He found that traumatic conditions in the present environment can trigger a release from the unconscious of the intolerably "bad" objects that the patient long ago repressed. When these bad objects "escape" from the unconscious, the patient is forced to confront early events that were too terrifying to maintain in consciousness. Like Winnicott, Fairbairn believed that the patient in such a situation is actually reliving an early and intensely painful situation. He said, "External situations . . . acquire . . . the significance of repressed situations involving relationships with bad objects. This phenomenon is accordingly not a phenomenon of projection, but one of 'transference'" (p. 76). Fairbairn felt that a controlled release of bad objects from the unconscious is devoutly to be desired in analysis, since the bad objects are such malignant elements of psychic structure, and their emergence in consciousness is the only way that the patient's libidinal bond to them can be dissolved.

Guntrip was largely in accord with Winnicott's and Fairbairn's views concerning the nature of transference phenomena. He pointed out, however, that the transference might also contain "unsatisfied legitimate longings for parental affection" (1969, 334), and that these might be disguised in sexual fantasies about the therapist. Guntrip warned that fantasies like these are not to be dismissed as mere infantile erotic wishes that the patient will have to outgrow. He saw them as "precious memories of a time when the parent–child relationship [was] good" and believed that patients who experienced such fantasies are regressing under "present-day strain" to thoughts of an early security that is now lost (p. 334).

This recalls Winnicott's discussion of the necessity of a "regression to dependence" which the analyst must welcome and facilitate. Guntrip's description of this phenomena conveys somewhat more explicitly the idea that the patient not only reexperiences an early intense dependence, but actually longs for the "holding" that the therapist may provide. This idea foreshadowed a key element in the work of Heinz Kohut, who eventually described in great and poignant detail the individual's longing for strong and loving selfobjects. Guntrip thought that while a patient might actually speak of wishing to be held in the therapist's lap, the therapist can adequately satisfy the longing that is being expressed by accepting and understanding the patient's need (1969, 335). This is, of course, identical to Winnicott's conception of how the analyst provides an adequate "holding environment" for the patient.

Kohut saw the analysis of transference as the "center of the analytic task" (1984, 201), and insisted that analysts' most "pivotal communications" to patients always concern transference phenomena (p. 192). He believed that transference relationships are founded upon particular, universal human needs and longings, but he was careful to distinguish his own model of transference from Freud's view that the analyst is the object of the patient's displaced instinctual urges. Kohut believed that the character of the transference is determined by something quite a bit grander than a drive for instinctual gratification. In his view, it is fundamentally shaped by the patient's need for selfobjects who stimulate and help to maintain the very "cohesion, vitality, strength, and harmony of the self" (p. 197).

Kohut identified three distinct "selfobject transferences" that arise as a result of frustrated developmental need. These include: (1) the mirror transference, in which the patient strives for the confirming and approving and hence self-maintaining responses of the selfobject; (2) the idealizing transference, in which the patient searches for a selfobject who is worthy and accepting of her need to merge with "an ideal of calmness and strength"; and (3) the twinship or alter ego transference, in which the patient seeks the "reassuring experience of essential likeness" (1984, 192–194).

Kohut maintained that the analysis of the predominant transference(s) manifested by a particular patient allows the analyst to identify the specific critical need(s) that are unfulfilled and likely well-concealed in the patient, and which undoubtedly are the source of great psychic pain. He said that the appearance of a selfobject transference in analysis is a sure sign that the individual's childhood needs for responsive selfobjects have not been entirely thwarted, and that the patient has managed to keep alive at least some meager hope of eventual self-realization and meaningful relatedness with other people. He viewed the psychoanalytic situation, in which the patient becomes the focus of the empathic attention of the analyst, as an ideal stimulus for the intensification of this hope and the evolution of the selfobject transference(s).

A theoretic wave, initiated by the British theorists, and flowing away from classical notions concerning the struggle between libido and the requirements of social order, reaches its highwater mark with Kohut's revision of the concept of transference. The psychotherapist is no longer at war with the patient's ego as it seeks to disguise the primitive urges of the id, but rather, becomes the advocate of the patient's self, as it struggles toward health by slowly revealing its damaged and fearful core.

Process and Technique

Classical psychoanalysis is founded on the premise that neurosis may be cured by exposing unconscious conflicts between the individual's urge for instinctual gratifications and the pressures of conscience and reality that oppose such gratification. The technique of psychoanalysis calls for the patient to "free associate" as a means of exposing these unconscious conflicts, and for the analyst to interpret resistance, transference, and id–ego struggle as these phenomena manifest themselves. Ideally, the analyst is to conduct herself according to the "rule of abstinence." This means that she must refrain from gratifying patients' demands for primitive id satisfactions, and must also avoid conforming to unconscious expectations that she will behave much as the parents did. The classical analyst, in other words, should serve as an uncontaminated screen for the patient's projections by maintaining an attitude of "neutrality" toward the patient, with his various demands and expectations.

British object relations theory and Self Psychology have revised many of the concepts that form the foundation of classical psychoanalysis and redefined the appropriate ends of analytic work, at least in regard to the therapy of certain types of personality disorder. These two approaches also prescribe far different means for the achievement of these ends. Their understanding of the meaning of patients' demands for gratification from therapists and their ideas about how such demands ought to be handled by a therapist are dramatically different from those of Freud.

Winnicott attributed a great deal of psychic suffering to parents' failures to respond adequately to their children's needs; therefore, he placed great importance on the therapist's capacity to understand, accept, and interpret these needs to patients. He believed that where parents are not reponsive to a child's most basic and critical needs, the true self that contains these needs will be repressed, and a false self will dominate the personality. Winnicott said that, in cases of severe false-self–true-self split, the main task of the analyst is to respond to patients' needs as would an "ordinary devoted mother" ([1956] 1975, 302), thus permitting the emergence of the true self. Failure to do so will result in "a reproduction of the environmental failure situation which stopped the processes of self growth" ([1954a] 1975, 288).

Winnicott said that the analytic setting, by virtue of its reliability, and its intense focus on the patient, duplicates early mothering techniques and invites the patient to "regress to dependence." Believing that organized regressive episodes form the bases for new growth, Winnicott stressed that he was concerned not with a return to particular points in the instinctual life of the individual, but rather, "to good and bad points in the environmental adaptation to ego needs and id needs" ([1954a] 1975, 283). He believed that when parents fail in some profound way to adapt to a child's needs, this "failure situation" becomes "frozen" in the child's psyche, but that it can become unfrozen and be reexperienced later, in the context of an environment that *is* making adequate adaptation (e.g., in psychotherapy). He felt that it was necessary for patients to reexperience early states of intense need with the analyst and for the analyst to correct parental errors at this point by deeply understanding the need and conveying this understanding ([1954b] 1975, 261).

Winnicott said that the deep understanding of patient need is one aspect of "management in analysis." He stressed that management does not involve satisfaction of patients' whims, nor an avoidance of their demands for help by providing reassurance. Rather, it means countering the adaptational deficits of the parental home by providing what is most fundamentally needed by the patient. Khan, in his 1971 introduction to Winnicott's text noted that this might include "abstention from intrusion by interpretation, and/or a sensitive body-presence in the person, and/or letting the patient move around and just be and do what he needs to" (p. xxvi).

Above all, for Winnicott, management seems to mean "holding" the patient in the secure grasp of the analyst's understanding and acceptance. This understanding and acceptance—proffered in the midst of what is, for the patient, a very painful, very frightening, regression to dependence—makes it possible for the patient to stop protecting the needy true self through the device of a false self, and permits a "new progression of the individual processes which had stopped". As the individual so progresses, she is able to feel anger about early environmental failure, and to express this anger in the present. In fact, in time, all the repressed feelings of the true self can be realized with "genuine vitality and vigor." In this sense, regression leads to a "new sense of self" ([1954a] 1975, 287).

Winnicott observed that communication with the true self in psychotherapy is also facilitated when the analyst directly addresses the condition of the self by pointing to its critical deficits, including its nebulous state, or its lack of knowledge. He found this approach to be much more useful than a prolonged analysis of ego-defense mechanisms, since the patient is, after all, devoted to the proposition that the false self is the real, total self, and will therefore cooperate endlessly with a therapist who sees the defensive layers of the personality as the most important aspect of the patient. Winnicott thought that real progress in psychotherapy can be made only as the therapist reaches out to the needy true self behind the defenses.

Winnicott saw that as therapists strive to adapt to patients' needs by understanding and addressing the needs of the true self, they inevitably make mistakes. Winnicott believed that an analysis and working through of these mistakes can be extremely valuable in psychotherapy. His statement that patients "use" the analyst's errors anticipated Kohut's later observation that, while an analyst's "optimal failures" will make the patient retreat, temporarily, from the analyst, an analytic investigation of this phenomenon can make the patient's self more resilient and lead to the development of new self structure.

Winnicott believed that patients become intensely angry and "act out" over seemingly small errors of judgment on the part of their therapists, because these failures are used by patients as a way of being angry about past failures of parental adaptation. The past failures are too threatening to face and react to, but the present failures can be perceived and encompassed, so that the patient feels able to be angry about them in the present. In Winnicott's view, patients' resistance or acting out always means that the analyst has made a mistake, "or in some detail has behaved badly," and he believed that the resistance will remain until the analyst discovers the error, analyzes it, and uses it. He warned that the therapist who defends himself against the patient's anger deprives a patient of the "opportunity for being angry about a past failure just where anger was becoming possible for the first time" ([1955] 1975, 298). He suggested that, instead, the analyst work toward discovering the error and deducing what was really needed by the patient at the point at which the error was made. He said that this will help the therapist and the patient to understand what went wrong in the original environmental failure situation and will produce a sense of relief in the patient. He felt that it also can lead to "a new sense of self in the patient" ([1954a] 1975, 290), though he did not explain why this should be so.

Winnicott's notes on analytic technique are principally concerned with the reclamation of the true self. Fairbairn also believed that human needs and object-longing (in the form of the libidinal ego) must be liberated from the unconscious in the course of analysis. Moreover, he felt that an analyst must somehow coax a schizoid patient into releasing his internalized and repressed bad objects, or at least reduce the active struggle between various structural components of the patient's psyche.

Winnicott suggested that analysts avoid preoccupation with their patients' ego-defenses, and Fairbairn also found that, in cases of severe psychic splitting, interpretations at the level of id gratification are of little avail. He found that it is far more productive to talk to patients about their object-relationships, "including of course, relationships with internalized objects" ([1943] 1981, 74). He said that all libidinal striving, or efforts to meet one's needs through object-relationships, should be represented to the patient as the result of love, and therefore as fundamentally good and healthy.

Fairbairn felt that any explicit reference to libidinal "badness" in psychotherapy should be reserved for those cases in which the patient has cathected a "bad" object. (When Fairbairn refers to an object as "bad," he usually means that the object is unavailable or abusive.) Fairbairn's idea that all libidinal striving is basically good and loving and object-directed, that badness resides not in the nature of the need but in the nature of the object, clashes with Freud's conception of libido as always sexual, as frequently primitive in its expression, and as emanating from an id that is by definition at odds with the dictates of reality and conscience. Thus, Fairbairn approached his patients with the idea that interpretations involving the concept of guilt should be applied only to situations in which they were involved with bad objects, and should never be used to convey the idea that a particular need is primitive or inappropriate. He also felt that the analyst should usually be cautious about accusing patients of aggressive intent against objects, since it exacerbates their sense of being "bad." It will be remembered that schizoid patients have internalized bad objects and feel pervasively "bad" anyway, and tend to use guilt as a defense against releasing their bad objects. Therefore, interpretations about aggression against objects can serve to reinforce a patient's defenses, rather than to penetrate them.

Though Fairbairn saw the analyst's benevolent attitude toward libidinal striving as an essential therapeutic factor, he believed that bad objects will finally be released from the patient's unconscious only if the analyst has managed to become a good object for the patient. Once again, Fairbairn felt that the deepest source of resistance in psychotherapy is the patient's fear of releasing bad objects. He believed that the analyst must provide patients with a deep sense of security and safety in which to release the internal "devils" by supplying them with a good object relationship. Fairbairn's idea that the therapist must become a "good" object to patients who have been surrounded by neglectful and abusive "bad" objects seems quite close to Winnicott's view that the therapist must create a "holding environment" that avoids the adaptational sins of the parents and restores the patient's hope, trust, and selfhood.

Harry Guntrip's perspective on analytic technique included Winnicott's ideas about the necessity of recovering the true, fearridden self through a regression to dependence in psychotherapy, and also incorporated Fairbairn's idea that the intense libidinal attachments of the patient to bad objects must be overcome in treatment. In addition he culled the writings of Winnicott and Fairbairn and deeply mined his own clinical experiences to provide a vivid and detailed account of the subjective state of the schizoid self, one that is extremely helpful to the clinician who seeks to understand and mitigate its longing. His eloquent attempt to distinguish what the analyst must *do* for the patient, and what the analyst must *be* to the patient in order for treatment to succeed brings much greater clarity and depth to such concepts as the holding environment and the analyst as a good object. His work on this issue is an elaborate precursor of Kohut's conception of the analyst as an empathic and idealizable selfobject for the patient.

Guntrip conceived of psychotherapy as progressing through three stages, or levels. The first is concerned primarily with the analysis of oedipal conflicts, the second is taken up with examination of the "schizoid compromises" in personal relations, while the third level, of "radical" psychotherapy, consists of a regression to dependence in which the "lost heart of the total self" reemerges and begins to grow once again. Guntrip said that in this third stage, the analyst gains real contact with the "terrified infant in retreat from life and hiding in his inner citadel." He quoted Fairbairn's observation that watching such a patient struggle between the intense fear of, and the desperate need for, human relationships is like watching "a timid mouse, alternately creeping out of the shelter of his hole to peep at the world of outer objects and then beating a hasty retreat" (1969, 282–283).

The fear of contacting outer objects is, for Guntrip as it is for Fairbairn, not just a fear that one will encounter further abuse and neglect. It is also a fear of relinquishing the "restrictive, oppressive, persecutory, inhibiting" bad objects of childhood that are installed in the psyche:

> ... when [the patient] gets over negative transference, i.e., the fear of meeting his bad parents again in his therapist, his fear of losing them remains so great that he will regard the analyst as someone who is going to rob him of his parents, even though it is also true that he looks to the analyst to rescue him from them. He will then face an awful period in which, if he loses his internal bad objects while not yet feeling sure enough that his therapist will adequately replace them, he will feel that he is falling between two stools, or as one patient vividly expressed it, "plunging into a mental abyss of black emptiness." It takes the patient a very long time really to feel that the therapist can be and is a better parent with respect to giving him a relationship in which he can become his own true self. Long after he is consciously and intellectually persuaded that this is so, the child deep within cannot feel it. (1969, 344)

Guntrip said that the patient undergoing this kind of regression, in which the basic conflict state is finally bared, feels despairing and hopeless, and periodically retreats back into a state of resistance (schizoid compromise). He believed that the patient at this stage is hampered in attempts at recovery not only by deeply embedded persecutory fears, but also by the existence of an "undeveloped weak infantile state." He postulated "a vicious circle in which the fears block ego development and the weak ego remains over susceptible to fears." He said that, "Psychotherapy has somehow to provide a new security in which a new growth can begin" (1969, 285).

Guntrip felt that the principal therapeutic factor in the recovery of schizoid patients "lies in what the therapist 'is,' what he is 'being' unselfconsciously in relation to the patient." He suggested that training analyses should aim not at the students' mastery of technique, but rather at helping students to become "whole or integrated" and "capable of effecting a real relationship through genuine care for and understanding of the patient" (1969, 312). He described psychotherapy as a "living personal relationship" and said that "No one is going to lay bare their intolerable hidden distress to satisfy someone's scientific curiosity. They will only do so if they become steadily convinced that we will stand by them and in the end relieve their misery" (1969, 322).

Guntrip thought that the patient's need for the therapist transcends the impulses of infantile eroticism, that the patient has "realistic emotional needs" that are "none the less realistic for emerging...in immature forms." Like Winnicott and Fairbairn, Guntrip believed that when such needs emerge, they reflect "that level of...unconscious childhood life which the analysis has reached and opened up," and that the success of psychotherapy depends on the therapist's ability to satisfy these basic longings:

> The patient's infantile ego can only grow in a genuine object-relationship. If the therapist persists in being, in reality, a merely objective scientific intelligence with no personal feeling for the patient, he will repeat on the patient the original emotional trauma suffered at the hands of parents, which laid the foundations of the illness. (1969, 335)

Because he placed such emphasis on the need for therapists to satisfy patients' needs for caring and loving relatedness to objects, and because this idea conflicts with traditional conceptions of an appropriately "abstinent" analytic attitude toward patients, Guntrip found it necessary to closely examine the implications of the patient's dependency on the therapist. His conclusion was that "the undermined basic ego" must be accepted for what it is, and that this does not constitute indulgence of childishness in the patient (1969, 287). He did note that while the patient's libidinal ego longs for such acceptance, the antilibidinal ego in the person hates the fact that another part of the self longs for help, and hates receiving any help. He found that if the patient senses that the therapist is also on the defensive against deep neediness in the patient, these needs will be forced to the surface of the personality, and the patient will become demanding and manipulative toward the analyst (the parent surrogate) who is behaving in a rejecting way. If, on the other hand, the analyst accepts and helps the child inside the patient, it is the antilibidinal ego that is flushed into the open, and the patient's most profound conflict—the fear of, and resistance against, dependency—is exposed. Guntrip believed that analysis of this problem is the the only sure path to recovery for the patient.

Guntrip summarized his ideas about technique and patient management by saying that, for schizoid patients, three things form a basis for recovery. First of all, such patients require "a relationship of a parental order which is sufficiently reliable and understanding to nullify the result of early environmental failure" (1969, 287). He thought that the parent-figure that is sought in these cases is needed mainly as "a protector against gross anxiety," and should be a purely supportive, protective reassuring love" that can allow one to exist with a sufficient sense of security (p. 336). Here, Guntrip's description of the truly therapeutic analyst clearly points toward the mirroring, idealizable qualities that Kohut later found to be essential in the growth-enhancing selfobject.

Guntrip also found that patients need an analysis of the many ways in which their needs for love and reassurance were thwarted by the parents and others in the original family group. Like Winnicott, Guntrip believed that such understanding is achieved primarily through analysis of transference phenomena. This is also a theme that will find full expression in Kohut's work.

Finally, Guntrip was certain that the real curative work of

analysis occurs through the medium of a regression to dependence that the therapist can understand and, in fact, welcome.
In the context of such a regression, the patient

> begins at first dimly, to feel that what he really needs is the
> basically non-erotic love of a stable parent in and through which
> the child grows up to possess an individuality of his own, a ma-
> turing strength of selfhood through which he becomes separate
> without feeling "cut off," and the original relationship to parents
> develops into adult friendship.... [this] issue is the most difficult
> therapeutic problem, and in this case the psychotherapist must
> be the kind of person who can relate to the patient in a way that
> enables him to find his own reality and experience a true "ego-
> birth and growth" in a way he could not do with his parents. This
> is something far deeper than questions about the satisfactions or
> conflicts concerning instinctive needs. They are subordinate as-
> pects of a total self, mature or immature. Here we are concerned
> with the possession of a meaningful self as distinct from a mere
> psychic existence which has lost its primary unity. In pursuit of
> this, the psychotherapist must be able to support the patient with
> unfailing care and understanding while leaving him free to be-
> come his own unique self in an "on the level" relationship....
> ... The therapist must now sense, not the patient's repressed
> conflicts but his unevoked potentialities for personal relationship
> and creative activity, and enable him to begin to feel "real." (1969,
> 336)

Guntrip's thinking about the therapist's attitude toward the
patient's deepest needs emphasizes the provision of genuine understanding and acceptance, but suggests that something more
is required as well. In the passage quoted above, Guntrip begins
to make the point that the therapist must really appreciate the
patient's individuality, and must approach the patient's growth
as an individual from a mainly non-self-interested posture. This
Guntrip referred to as "true parental love" that "does not regard
the child as a nuisance, or as a piece of clay to be moulded, or
as there to fit in merely with the parents' convenience or to fulfill
their ambitions for themselves, or what not" (1969, 351). Guntrip

felt that this "disinterested personal love" was the sine qua non of Fairbairn's "good object" and hence, of the good therapist. It is also a central feature of Kohut's program for the restoration of the self.

Heinz Kohut believed that psychological health depends solely on the integrity of the structure of the self. His idea that flaws in the self-structure are attributable to disturbances in the early relationship between the self and its primary selfobjects led him to emphasize the curative power of an analyst's empathic understanding and acceptance of the patient as an individual.

Kohut outlined a three-step process for the analysis and restoration of the self that is quite similar in spirit to the tripartite model proposed by Guntrip, but which is far broader and richer in content than the latter. Kohut said that a self psychological analysis proceeds from the analysis of defenses through the unfolding of the selfobject transferences and culminates in "the opening of a path of empathy between self and selfobject" (1984, 66). It should be noted that a principal difference between Kohut's conception of the the three phases of psychotherapy and Guntrip's formulation is that Kohut saw oedipal problems primarily in terms of the nature of changes in the self that typically occur during this period of development, and believed that oedipal pathology is the result of faulty responses from the parents toward the child's oedipal self. Since he believed that oedipal pathology is an aspect of self-pathology and that its therapeutic manifestation occurs in the context of a selfobject transference, he did not posit a discrete phase of oedipal analysis as a prelude to the analysis of the self.

Guntrip saw the schizoid compromise, in its varied forms, as the individual's main line of defense against dependency and emotional intimacy. He felt that a detailed analysis of this defense necessarily precedes the organized, controlled regression that paves the way for a period of regrowth. Kohut conceived of defensive structures in the psyche in a broader, more varied way than Guntrip, but like Guntrip believed that these defenses are designed to protect the gravely compromised and highly vulnerable self. He felt that an important portion of psychotherapy must be devoted to an analysis of these defenses, in the sense that both therapist and patient must come to understand how they operate and the forces that compel their existence.

The British theorists viewed regression as an aspect of transference, and felt that early, deeply repressed object relationships, and the affects associated with them, must be reexperienced in therapy if the individual is to progress psychologically. Kohut also believed that repressed or split-off object relationships and needs are remobilized in the relationship between analyst and analysand. He called this process the selfobject transference. Kohut's conceptualization of the selfobject, and his effort to describe and differentiate the varieties of selfobject transferences that are possible, provided us with a far more sophisticated and systematized understanding of regressive phenomena in psychotherapy. Kohut, as we have seen, believed that the analysis of the particular selfobject transference is a critical stage of therapy that provided a basis for understanding the patient in the deepest possible way.

During the third phase of the self psychological analysis, the empathic link between the self and its new, more responsive selfobject is forged, and the nuclear self can begin to implement its "intrinsic program of action" (1984, 42). This phase is analagous, in many ways, to Guntrip's third phase, in which "the lost heart of the total self" is recovered in consciousness, and can begin to grow again. Kohut, however, in his effort to understand how the self can be freed for new growth, undertook an elaborate exploration of the phenomena of empathy and the impact of empathic understanding on the self. He defined empathy as "vicarious introspection"—the "capacity to think and feel oneself into the inner life another person" (1984, 82). While the British theorists realized that the therapist's understanding is important in imparting a vitally necessary sense of security to an embryonic and struggling self, it was Kohut who insisted that the empathic responsiveness of another person is required for the development of the self—that it stimulates sharper definition, further structuralization, and greater cohesion of the self. His work on this issue has greatly enhanced our understanding of the curative factors in psychotherapy.

According to Kohut, it is also during the third phase that the empathic bond between the therapist and the patient supplants the attachment of the self to the "archaic selfobjects" of childhood. Kohut's conception of the archaic selfobject is quite close to Fairbairn's conception of the bad object, and Kohut also had the idea that a successful therapy will result, not in freedom from object ties, but in an increased ability to make attachments to responsive, rewarding objects.

Kohut believed that in general analysis proceeds toward the goal of self-restoration through the therapist's noncensorious interpretation of transference phenomena and reconstructions of childhood traumata that resulted in damage to the self. These interpretations and reconstructions, however, are effective only if they occur in the context of a "basic in-tuneness" between the patient and the analyst. This "in-tuneness," for Kohut, consists of the therapist's understanding and acceptance of the patient's needs for adequately responsive selfobjects. Like, the British theorists, Kohut felt that the emergence of these needs in therapy is the key to recovery, and that to dismiss or reject them is a grave clinical error. He advised therapists to:

> explain these needs [and their frustration] in a noncensorious way, that is, ... explain them as primary needs that [have] not been responded to in childhood, that have gone into hiding, and whose transference reactivation is to be welcomed. ... [realize], in other words, that the remobilization of these needs constitutes a positive analytic development ... that it would be an error to reject them by interpreting them either as unwelcome defensive maneuvers, as attempts to escape the painful confrontation of anxiety- and guilt-provoking aggressive and sexual drive-wishes,

or as a clinging to outdated drive-pleasures that must be opposed
by the reality principle and the strictures of adult reality. (1984,
84)

Kohut explained his disdain for confrontations about patients'
defensiveness and demandingness by saying that they are frequently "trite, superfluous, and ... patronizing"; he charged that
they "may repeat the essential trauma of childhood in a way
that is especially harmful to the progress of the analysis" (1984,
173). He added that:

> By failing to acknowledge the validity and legitimacy of the pa-
> tient's demands for development-enhancing selfobject responses
> ... the analyst fails the patient in the same way the parent had
> failed—often the more responsive parent to whom the child hope-
> fully turned after the parent whose responses were even more flat,
> more severely distorted, and the like had failed him. That it may
> occasionally be helpful to an analysand ... to hear from the an-
> alyst that old grievances, however valid and legitimate, must
> finally be relinquished, and that new and more responsive
> selfobjects must be sought in the present, goes without saying. . . .
> however ... I have come to the conclusion that confrontations
> should be used sparingly. . . . they provide nothing that is not al-
> ready provided by the realities of adult life. (1984, 173)

Kohut believed it is the first responsibility of the analyst to
understand the psychic life of the patient, especially the patient's
deep need and longing for responsive and affirming selfobjects.
It is essential that the analyst

> verbalize to the patient that he has grasped what the patient feels;
> ... describe the patient's inner state to the patient, thus demon-
> strating to him that he has been "understood," that is, that an-
> other person has been able to experience, at least in
> approximation, what he himself experienced, whether, for ex-
> ample, the experience in question is one of inner emptiness and
> depression, or of pride and enhanced self-esteem. (1984, 176–177)

Although Kohut believed that, in some cases, the analyst has to devote herself, for long periods of time, simply to understanding the inner life of the patient, he also felt that in the long run analysis will progress successfully only if the analyst also explains to the patient how the events and relationships of childhood have produced these particular psychological experiences. Kohut called the two-step process of understanding and explaining the "basic therapeutic unit." (1984, 96) Understanding, or empathy, Kohut believed, "constitutes the essence of psychoanalytic cure," but the explanation is necessary in order to deepen the patient's own "empathic-accepting grasp of himself" and "strengthen [his] trust in the reality and reliability of the empathic bond that is being established between him and his analyst" (p. 105). Kohut also found that while empathy leads to increased structuralization of the self, accurate, well-timed interpretations seem to "implant the wholesome . . . experience of having been understood into a broader area of the upper layers of the analysand's mind," making it available for recall during the important period of working through (p. 106).

Kohut saw, as did Winnicott, that an analyst will inevitably err in her efforts to understand the patient and to explain the roots of the patient's difficulties. Kohut believed that nontraumatic failures, including empathic error, on the part of an adequately functioning selfobject are actually necessary for the growth of the self. Like Winnicott, he felt that the therapist's handling of such errors is a key to patient recovery.

Kohut observed that when the basic in-tuneness between analyst and patient is disrupted by unavoidable, yet temporary and therefore nontraumatic empathy failures, the patient is confronted with an "optimal frustration" (1984, 70). This sort of empathic failure, or an inaccurate or improper interpretation, causes the patient to retreat temporarily from the relationship with the therapist into a psychic engagement with the archaic selfobjects of childhood. For example, a patient disappointed and hurt by a therapist's failure to understand some important emotional event, might try to compensate for this disappointment by merging with an idealized omnipotent selfobject, or seeking immediate and perfect mirroring from the analyst or some other important figure. Sometimes when Ed was devastated by a rejection from a girlfriend, I failed to empathize with his feelings of loss and worthlessness and instead urged him to try to alter his masochistic posture with women. On one occasion, I compounded my empathic error by asking why he was consistently attracted only to women who seemed to be compulsive abandoners. This humiliated Ed, and he flew into a rage and began to curse me. This was his way of demonstrating to me, in no uncertain terms, that he desperately needed me to reestablish my empathic bond with him. Kohut said that in such situations, the analyst must recognize the patient's retreat, and search for the mistake that precipitated it. When the mistake is discovered, the therapist must nondefensively acknowledge it, and then explain to the patient why the mistake led to a frightened retreat. In this way, and only in this way, can the channel of empathy between the therapist and the patient be reopened. Once it is, the two can proceed with the primary mission of the therapy, which is to help the patient relinquish the destructive self–selfobject relationships of childhood, and to take refuge in self-enhancing bonds with new, adequately empathic selfobjects. In chapter 6, I describe how I worked through my empathic errors with Ed.

Kohut was certain that nontraumatic empathic failures by the analyst, when handled properly, lead to "the acquisition of self-esteem-regulating psychological structure" in the patient (1984, 67). This certainty was rooted in his belief that many of the analyst's comforting and confidence-inspiring qualities, including the ability to sustain empathic connectedness in the face of a patient's disappointment, retreat, and aggression, are eventually incorporated by the patient, becoming "part of [the] psychological equipment" (1977, 32). Kohut called this incorporative process "transmuting internalization" (1971, p. 49).

Fairbairn and Guntrip knew that the analyst must become a good object for the patient so that the need and longing of the self can be safely experienced and revealed to the outer world. The concept of transmuting internalization goes quite a bit beyond the idea that the analyst creates a secure environment for the recovery and restoration of the self. It suggests that the "good" qualities of the therapist—compassion, calmness, strength, and the capacity for empathic connectedness—can be taken in by the patient and form in him the foundation for a more compassionate, self-accepting, unanxious, resilient, and empathic self.

Since Kohut believed that essential features of the analyst's self are eventually internalized by the patient, he felt, as Guntrip did, that the state of the therapist's self has great impact on the ultimate outcome of psychotherapy. Guntrip addressed the importance of the analyst as a "real object," not just a "projection screen" (1969, 335). Kohut, too, saw the analyst as a "significant human presence," with an influence on the patient that transcends "distorting countertransferences" (1984, 37). He said that the analytic situation, with its intense, exclusive focus on the patient's inner life, can never really be "neutral":

> On the contrary, it is a situation that, in its psychological impact on us, is the very opposite of neutral—indeed it is a situation that may be said to provide us with the most crucial emotional experience for human psychological survival and growth: the attention of a selfobject milieu, that is, a human surrounding that, via empathy, attempts to understand and participate in our psychological life. And the quality of the understanding that is achieved, its relative accuracy, inaccuracy, insufficiency, or oppressiveness, is an immanent quality of the analytic situation, not an adventitious admixture to it. (1984, 37)

Kohut stressed that the analyst must be able to respond in a natural, relaxed way to patients, and must provide the sort of responsiveness "to be expected, on the average, from persons who have devoted their lives to helping others." This "average expectable environment," Kohut said, cannot be provided by therapists whose theoretical biases or defects of self cause them to try to behave like a "programmed computer" that restricts its actions to giving correct and accurate interpretations" (1977, 252). On the contrary, the analyst must be a "lively emotional presence" in therapy and free of any rigid conception of mental health that might stunt the patient's growth as an individual (1984, 170–171). While these qualities are affected by the therapist's theoretic orientation, they are also dependent on the cohesiveness, strength, and vitality of the therapist's own self.

Summary

The successful therapeutic process outlined by the British theorists and by Kohut aims at the liberation, affirmation, and consolidation of the patient's self, and the loosening of its ties to destructive objects in the inner, as well as outer, world. It is conducted by a relatively active and emotionally responsive psychotherapist who explicitly addresses and genuinely accepts the terror, defensiveness, and neediness of the patient's real, empathically deprived, perhaps abused, self. It is this issue—the origin of the patient's need and the appropriate therapeutic response to that need—that most clearly distinguishes British Object Relations theory and Self Psychology from classical analysis.

The British school and Self Psychology both hold that the therapist's compassion for and deep understanding of patients' longing for human connectedness and emotional support creates an atmosphere of safety for the patient. Winnicott called this "the holding environment." In this psychologically secure situation, patients are free to experience, in consciousness, previously repressed or split off states of need. They are also filled with the hope they need if they are to abandon their ties to the destructive objects of childhood and to seek fulfillment in new relationships. According to Kohut, the therapist's calm acceptance of all aspects of a patient's self is internalized by the patient and becomes the structural foundation for greater self-esteem and self-empathy.

The first manifestations of the patient's need in psychotherapy typically occur in the context of regressive episodes, or as Kohut put it "spontaneously occurring selfobject transferences" (1984, 66). This means that the patient reexperiences early conditions of need that were unsatisfied, punished, or perhaps misunderstood by parents. When these needs are felt and expressed in relation to the therapist, it is the therapist's task to meet them in a more helpful and constructive way than the parents did. Though the therapist will not be able to satisfy all of the patient's longing, accurate empathy for the suffering and the triumphs of the patient's self will strengthen and unify it.

6
CLINICAL STRATEGIES
FOR USE WITH
ADULT CHILDREN

ONE OF my patients entered therapy in her early twenties in order to work through the suicide of her alcoholic and tranquilizer-dependent mother, who had committed suicide when my patient was 15. This young woman could never adequately mourn her mother's loss, because her father was completely unable to confront his own grief and deep sense of guilt over his wife's addiction and suicide. He blocked every attempt by his daughter to express sadness, rage, or fear about her mother's death.

This patient had received some brief psychotherapy for anxiety attacks at her university's counseling center, but she agreed with her therapist there that she needed to tackle some relatively deep issues about her mother that could never be resolved in a short-term therapy. The patient was an extremely intelligent and articulate young woman who worked in a paraprofessional helping capacity herself. Since she was so knowledgeable about mental health work and since she had found her previous psychotherapy so helpful, she was confused and troubled by the considerable anxiety that she experienced before meeting with me each week. Her extreme fearfulness made it difficult for her to share deeper feelings with me or even to look at me very often during our sessions. During the early months of this young woman's therapy, she had a dream that explained this intense fear.

In the dream, the patient showed her mother a small and fragile caged bird that was the daughter's pet. The mother reached into the cage, and the patient thought, "She is going to pet the bird." Instead of petting the bird, however, the mother grabbed the bird and crushed it.

This simple, but terribly disturbing dream revealed the entire purpose of this patient's psychotherapy as well her terror of embarking upon it. Actually, the most fundamental purpose of psychotherapy with any adult child is to open a hidden, imprisoned, and extremely fragile part of the self, and convince it to allow itself to be touched by another person. But these patients all fear, as this one obviously did, that if they open the door to the heart of the self, it will be crushed by the therapist, just as it was nearly crushed by the insensitivity, abuse, or betrayal of the parent(s).

Self Psychology and British Object Relations Theory prescribe a form of psychotherapy that searches out the hidden heart of the self in order to unify the psyche and allow the self to begin a new period of growth. They advocate an explicit clinical focus on the condition of vital psychic structures, especially their incompleteness, fragmentation, divisiveness, and defensiveness. Kohut, of course, believed that psychic structure is self structure. He proposed that all psychotherapeutic interventions should address, and aim at increasing, the cohesion, vitality, and harmony of the self.

The British theorists, and Kohut, believed that the fundamental condition of the self, as well as transient self states, are largely dependent on the quality of the relationships between the self and its objects. They held that impairments of the self can be significantly reduced, if the therapist responds to the frustrated longings of the self as the parents could not—with understanding, acceptance, and a willingness to work toward their ultimate resolution.

This chapter applies the tenets of British Object Relations Theory and Self Psychology to self disorders in adult children of alcoholics. It advances several general principles of psychotherapy that are designed to address, and redress, the critical failures of the alcoholic home. It should be noted that, while each of these principles describes a relatively discrete aspect of psychotherapy with adult children, they are all ultimately concerned with the provision of the calm, empathic, and strong selfobject environment that was largely unavailable to the patient during childhood.

The Healing Environment: A Psychological Safety Net

The adult child's feeling of psychological safety in psychotherapy depends on the therapist's capacity to convince the patient that he will not be subjected to the sorts of traumatic disappointments that were commonplace occurrences in the alcoholic home. Therapeutic error, as we have learned, is an unavoidable feature of clinical practice in psychology, and while many adult children are greatly disturbed even by the therapist's relatively small failures, these events can usually be turned to good use in the psychotherapy. As Kohut pointed out, if the therapist adequately analyzes and interprets the nature and the consequences of clinical error, mistakes can actually constitute "optimal frustrations" that strengthen the self structure. However, a constructive outcome is possible only if the therapist's errors remain nontraumatic in nature and frequency.

Each patient has special sensitivities to particular kinds of disappointment, of course. These individual differences depend in large measure on specific traumas to which the patient has been subjected in childhood, and the amount and quality of support that the patient originally received in attempting to deal with these traumas. In general, however, there are certain basic conditions that must be met for every adult child in treatment, if the therapist is to become a "good object" who represents a viable alternative to the internalized abusive objects of the patient's childhood.

> *Principle Number One*: The healing environment must be characterized by emotional warmth and responsiveness. The therapist must display an appreciation of the patient's basic worth and an acceptance of the patient's individuality.

As Kohut observed, a therapist's response to patients should be characterized by the sort of warm responsiveness to be expected from an individual whose professional life is devoted to understanding and helping others. Therapists are not mere "projection screens," but people who have enormous importance as "real" objects. Beyond analysis and interpretation, the "real" qualities of the therapist—warm interest, caring, and respect for the patient as an individual—are the things that rekindle the hope for the future that has been mostly suffocated in a neglectful and abusive alcoholic home. The patient will excuse many instances of empathic failure if these mistakes occur in the context of the therapist's obvious regard for the patient and the work. Not caring is an obvious clinical sin. Miller (1985) noted, in his description of the psychological supervision that he received from Kohut, that Kohut also felt that it was detrimental to *pretend* not to care in the interest of maintaining one's "analytic neutrality" (p. 22).

Many adult children of alcoholics have been reared by parents with deeply flawed self structures and critically impaired self-esteem. As Kohut pointed out, parents who suffer from severe self-disorders are unable to mirror (affirm and support) distinctive and healthy aspects of a child's unfolding self. An alcoholic and an enabling spouse are likely to thwart the natural course of self-development in a child by using a son or daughter as a container for parental self-loathing or by mirroring only those qualities of the child's self that are necessary to bind the parent's anxiety and stabilize the parent's self. The parent with a self-disorder may also try to crush elements in the child's self that threaten the parent's fragile narcissism. The therapist should look for opportunities to support the patient's self-esteem and to encourage the expression and growth of parts of the patient's self that were damaged and driven into hiding by parental neglect or aggression.

Jack

It was always clear to Jack that his parents expected him to excel in school and at sports, and that they were disappointed whenever he failed to turn in a first-rate performance. However, both parents were relatively cool and restrained each time he reached a new pinnacle of achievement in either realm. Their lack of enthusiasm on these occasions convinced Jack that his own feelings of excitement and self-satisfaction about his achievements was somehow "wrong" and inappropriately prideful. He tried to subdue these feelings, and in time he came to feel like a machine whose continued superb functioning was more a matter of programming than unique capacity and monumental effort. He began to believe that his triumphs deserved no special notice.

Jack's achievements in school often received very special notice from his teachers and peers, however. For example, in junior high school he received a schoolwide award for citizenship. Because Jack was accustomed to diminishing the importance and personal meaning of these sorts of honors, he planned not to mention the award to his parents. However, the obvious excitement that his teachers and fellow students felt about his achievement convinced him that it was, in fact, something very special, and he finally decided to tell his mother what had happened. She didn't praise Jack when he told her the news, nor did she try to share in the pleasure he felt about the recognition he had received at school. Instead, she told Jack that she and his father had both won this award when they were Jack's age,

and she began to reminisce about how she had felt on the day she had taken the prize. Jack's excitement about his own accomplishment was crushed.

Jack's parents needed his success as a buttress for their own sagging self-esteem. The emotional inhibition and self-preoccupation resulting from their own illnesses precluded a real empathic response to their son. They felt no joy over Jack's occasional deep pleasure and intellectual excitement about his studies, or his own sense of gratification at receiving the admiration of others. His parents' failure to be truly touched by these parts of him left Jack feeling empty and futile about his academic endeavors. Still, he felt compelled to succeed—for them.

Interestingly, Jack retained feelings of excitement and vitality about sports. His father was also extremely devoted to sports and demonstrated interest and some degree of pride in Jack's athletic prowess. His father's ability to mirror this aspect of Jack's self undoubtedly helped it to continue to feel alive and important. On the day of a pivotal high school game, Jack was surprised and delighted to look into the stands and find both his parents in attendance. His father was usually too busy with work to attend these contests. Jack played a good game and was especially pleased to receive his father's praise for this performance. This pleasure turned to disappointment and hurt later on, however, when his mother, acting out of apparent envy over this moment of connectedness between Jack and his father, informed Jack that his father had fallen asleep in the stands early in the game and had actually missed most of the important play.

Jack coped with his parents' self-interested response to his achievements by concealing them. He was still, on occasion, dimly aware of feelings of pleasure connected with special things he accomplished and with the actual process of studying, working, or playing sports. He took pains to suppress and conceal these too, since he still felt they were wrong, or inappropriate in some way.

It is a testimony to the strength of Jack's split off, core self that he was able to embark on a career path that de-

viated sharply from the one his parents had plotted out for
him. It was inexplicable to him that he had done so, since
for a long time, he had been unable to feel any strong sense
of purpose or interest about his chosen work. When he felt
some spark of enthusiasm in school, or at work, or when
he received some special recognition or passed an academic
milestone, he was understandably reluctant to feel about
these events with me, or to even mention them to me. When
he did mention them, they were usually things or feelings
that had occurred weeks or months ago, and he was always
careful to preface his remarks by saying, "I know this isn't
really worth mentioning, but ... " or "I don't know if this
is important to say, but ... "

I always assured Jack that such things were *crucially
important* for him to raise in therapy, since they were sig-
nals from the inner man, the core Jack, about who he was
apart from his parents' needs. I also made every effort to
express pleasure that *he* was beginning, once again, to take
pleasure from the work he had chosen for himself. I often
referred to him as a "scholar" and a "talented clinician,"
in an attempt to sharpen those aspects of Jack's self that
seemed most often to give him genuine pleasure. This always stimulated Jack's fear that he might become prideful
or hopeful about some achievement that "amount[ed] to
nothing, really." Very gradually, however, my mirroring of
these essential qualities strengthened them and helped
Jack to overcome, in great measure, his inhibitions about
sharing these parts of himself with me. He also became
better able to display his excitement about scholarly work
and clinical practice to selected colleagues and teachers
who were able to provide further mirroring.

Principle Number Two: The healing environment must be
a stable environment.

Unpredictability and unreliability are hallmarks of the alcoholic home, and many adult children consciously expect to en-

counter gross impulsivity in their therapists. It goes without saying that if the therapist does prove to be erratic or unreliable in some important way, frequently canceling or rescheduling appointments for example, or behaving in a seductive or dishonest fashion with the patient, there will be an immediate and deleterious effect on the work. Since many adult children defend themselves against parental instability by eschewing the passive, painful role of victim in favor of becoming an active victimizer, it is common for adult children to respond to a therapist's instability by becoming unstable themselves. Thus, the adult child may begin skipping appointments, or may try to engage the therapist in some illicit behavior. The patient may withdraw from therapy altogether. (Of course, the patient may do any or all of these things without any provocation by the therapist. This issue is handled below, under Principle Five, which deals with patient defensiveness.)

If the patient cannot depend on the *emotional* stability and availability of the therapist, this, too, will be disturbing. For example, if the therapist's empathy for the patient often falters, and he frequently responds in an overly anxious or angry manner when the patient is defensive or behaves self-destructively, this will trigger a retreat by the patient. The patient may leave therapy, or, feeling psychologically annihilated by the therapist's intense response (which is subjectively experienced by the patient as punitive and disapproving), may try to retaliate in kind. The following case illustrates a patient's extreme sensitivity to my failure to maintain an unanxious and supportive holding environment for his own unpredictable and frightening emotionality. Since I recognized and understood my error in time, it did not reach traumatic proportions, but it easily could have, and I include it as an example of the sort of disturbing interaction that occurs repeatedly in work with adult children and which frequently provokes an impulsive and uncharacteristically punitive response from the therapist that vividly recalls a key parental failure and therefore proves to be an irrevocably traumatic disappointment for the patient. This vignette also illustrates transference phenomena and highlights a defensive structure typical of these patients. (The issues of transference and defense will be directly examined under Principles Four and Five.)

Ed

Ed's principal psychic nemeses were his propensity to intense and pervasive shame reactions and the recurrent states of profound inner emptiness that were the consequence of his failure to make attachments to adequately responsive and empathic objects. He habitually responded to feelings of shame and emptiness by dealing drugs, since this gave him a feeling of power and importance, and answered his loneliness by surrounding him with a band of admiring retainers and hopeful supplicants.

Early in our work, I responded to Ed's socially and psychologically destructive solutions to his emotional pain by anxiously pointing to the extreme dangerousness of his behavior, especially in light of the extremity of his present legal situation. His periods of "acting out" were invariably linked to yet another shame- and despair-inducing failure with a destructive lover, and I always interpreted this connection. These interventions were never helpful to Ed, and always provoked him to a rageful verbal assault on me. "You're pushing me to the wall!," he would bellow. "Nothing ever works for me, anyway. All anybody wants to do is get theirs. And that's all I'm going to care about. There's no love out there. There's no one that cares. You're not helping me. You're like all the others and you can just get off my back!"

I reacted to Ed's tirades with feelings of shame, guilt, and resentment. For me, there could be no more painful experience than that of being unhelpful and "just like all the rest." Certainly Ed was sufficiently insightful and psychologically minded to sense my psychic jugular. I had fleeting fantasies of terminating the therapy or staging an angry confrontation of my own against Ed.

I understood that I was failing Ed at these junctures, and I eventually understood how I was failing him. Ed's periods of panic and hopelessness seemed to be related to his extreme isolation from any realistic sort of help when he felt overwhelmed by his extensive academic and job-related responsibilities, as well as problems in his relationships with women. When Ed turned to his father for help at these times, he tended to be critical of Ed's problematic romantic relationships, and unwilling or unable to understand the pressure that Ed faced as he tried to balance his ambitions at school and work with his desperate need for companionship. What Ed had always needed, but failed to find in his father, was an appreciation for the depth of his loneliness, and a willingness to listen to and accept his longing. I was usually able to answer this need, but when I became extremely anxious about his masochism or his drug-dealing, I tended to deviate from my customary empathic course. When I did so, I effectively repeated his father's original traumatic failure to understand Ed's need for someone to understand and explicitly acknowledge the intense emotional pain that lay beneath his delinquent behavior.

Even when I finally understood the dynamics of my conflict with Ed, it was difficult for me to understand why my occasional failures to apprehend his need for support and understanding were felt as an attack by me, or why he was so completely unable, at such times, to hear any part of my warnings as an essentially caring effort to divert him from a self-destructive path. However, I eventually had a consultation with Ed's father, and after this meeting I was able to appreciate the extreme state of siege that Ed experienced when I anxiously confronted his self-destructiveness.

Ed's father was most concerned about his son's dangerous behavior and he was quite aware that his responses to Ed's requests for guidance and support in the midst of a crisis were usually motivated by extreme anxiety. He reported that, after each panicky effort to divert Ed from a self- destructive course of behavior, the relationship between father and son always suffered a dramatic deterioration. A pitched argument was likely to ensue, with Ed screaming obscenities at his father and accusing him of a variety of miserable failures, including ignorance, neglect, and so forth.

The father's response to these outbursts, which had begun to occur early in Ed's adolescence, was interesting. On several occasions the father had felt the urge to strike Ed but had never done so. Instead, he responded to Ed in kind, cataloguing all of the boy's vile failures as a son. As the father explained, "I figure, at those times, one of us is going to get blown away. It's him or me. And better him than me." This conversation helped me to understand Ed's desperate assault on my self-esteem when I committed an empathic error. The father's narcissistic balance was severely upset by Ed's attacks. Therefore, the father could not set aside his own feelings and be a parent to his son by soothing and reassuring him when Ed began to fragment under pressure. Indeed, the father had to shore up his own imperiled self by staging a counter-assault on his son. Ed brought this same "It's you or me" mentality to his dealings with me. If I appeared to falter under the pressure of his impending disintegration, it signaled real danger—not just that he would be left stranded and unsupported in his time of need, but that he would once again be the victim of an all out psychic assault. My interpretation of this process to Ed helped us to eliminate these kinds of anxious and angry confrontations from our own relationship. Further, it helped Ed to begin to identify similar breakdowns of communication and connectedness as they occurred in his relationships with other people. At this point he also began to separate from friends and lovers, who, like his father, felt compelled to protect themselves in a conflict by assaulting the very foundations of his self.

Principle Number Three: The healing environment must be characterized by openness to intellectual and emotional experience.

The fabric of the psychological safety net is also fashioned from the therapist's ability to model and inspire an attitude of emotional openness and intellectual curiousity in the therapy.

The alcoholic family, in its isolation and its ignorance about the disease of alcoholism, has usually been forced into a "conspiracy of silence" about the family's enormous struggle and pain. Black observed that the alcoholic family acts according to the motto, "Don't talk, don't trust, don't feel" (1981, 31). The adult child in psychotherapy is often deeply conflicted about exposing personal struggles and pains to the therapist. Very often, patients will unconsciously defend against such a conflict by failing to remember sensitive material or connect it with its associated affect in the therapist's presence. While it is often necessary to graciously and unanxiously weather a patient's protracted period of active ambivalence about emotional sharing, there is still much that the therapist can do to create a therapeutic atmosphere that is marked by an openness to affective and cognitive experience.

Enlarging the emotional experience of the patient. Since the alcoholic family has usually gone to great lengths to diminish the patient's affective life, the therapist will, by necessity, expend a great deal of effort in order to enlarge it. It is usually necessary, first of all, to help the patient to understand the familial roots of the difficulty with emotional sharing, and to prepare the patient for the possibility that a feeling of trust and ease about exposing the past, and the self, may take some time to acquire (see also Principle Five). Most adult children are ashamed when they are unable to produce rich, emotionally charged material for the therapist's edification. A patient may have to be repeatedly assured that the ongoing resolution of the ambivalence is, in itself, a necessary and valuable aspect of the work. The therapist's calm acceptance of conflicts involving emotional intimacy does much to free patients from the feeling that their true state of being can never be safely shared with the therapist, or anyone else.

When emotionally charged material does emerge during a

session, the therapist must be careful not to prematurely abridge or diminish the client's affective experience. There may be a temptation to do so, especially if the affect is intensely negative, and therefore very frightening to the therapist or the patient. However, the active expression of disturbing affects in therapy is generally a sign of the progressive strengthening of the therapeutic alliance. It is also an opportunity for the patient to undergo a constructive regression in which the previously unmet needs for a calm and integrating and supportive selfobject can be answered by the therapist, leading to an increased or enhanced structuralization of the patient's self. A therapist who genuinely believes that emotional expressiveness, even in a raw and intense form, represents therapeutic gain, can usually set aside fright, or some ill-conceived need to "protect" the patient, and attempt to empathize with the nature and source of the particular pain. This action will, generally, have a calming effect in and of itself. Such a therapist can also usually convince a patient that the emergence of the feelings during a session is a good sign, and the two can proceed to explore the affect, and its implications for the patient's psychodynamics and the patient's life.

Paul

Paul was particularly frightened by his recurrent and intense experiences of despair and hopelessness. The most frightening depressive episodes tended to occur on weekends, when he was deprived of the comforting structure of the work day and what were usually nominal, but psychically vital, interactions with his colleagues. He was often troubled by suicidal thoughts on the weekends, and frequently sought to relieve his agitation by attending a pornographic movie. He often rounded off these episodes by engaging in anonymous sex with either a female prostitute or a male stranger he encountered at the movies.

Paul and I discussed the connection between his feelings of emptiness, anxiety, and despair and what he referred to as his sexual "acting out." I suggested that the isolation of the weekends stirred in him the emotional memory of the isolation he experienced during childhood, and that, as this memory was stirred, he began to relive the hopelessness he must have felt then. This hopelessness was unbearable to him, and he tried to resolve it by making some connection with another human being. His attempts to connect with his father had been a dismal failure, so he was too frightened to try for a true, emotionally intimate, encounter with someone. Pornography and anonymous sex, were, for Paul, a "schizoid compromise" between real connectedness with others and total isolation from human interaction.

After I had interpreted this sequence to Paul several times, he began to have deeper experiences of despair during our actual sessions together. I viewed this as a constructive regression to dependency (or unfolding of the selfobject transference, discussed below). Paul was allowing me to see and care for the hurt and needy child within— the aspect of his self which had been forced, by the rejection from his father, to split away from the central, conscious sector of his psyche. Paul was frightened that he felt hopeless in my presence, because consciously he saw me as the only person who could deliver him from his despair. I told Paul that the emergence of these feelings in the sessions was actually an important sign of progress in the work and in our relationship. The only viable solution to his inner emptiness would be an increase in his ability to share with others the parts of himself that he had been hiding. This he was beginning to do with me. Paul was initially skeptical about this idea. A previous therapist had been strongly critical of Paul's depressive collapses, and, like Paul's father, had advised him to "act like a man," join some social groups, and begin to engage in constructive activity on the weekends. Though Paul had felt no gains from his work with this therapist, and had ended the treatment after a few months, he was inclined to believe that this therapist, like his father, knew him for the weakling he really was. He was afraid that I, on the other hand, was coddling him. However, as he began to reveal the depths of his despondency to me, his suicidal ideation diminished and the anon-

ymous sexual encounters disappeared entirely. These gains
were heartening to him.

After an extended period of working through Paul's feelings of despair in sessions together, he felt hopeful enough
about the prospect of contacting strong and supportive selfobjects that he was able to join Al-Anon and a sexual addictions support group that follows the format of the
Twelve Step programs. He began to attend these groups
almost daily and to build satisfying relationships with
peers as well as older adults who made real efforts to re-
parent him.

Educating the patient. The provision to patients of accurate
information and education about the pervasive and penetrating
effects of parental alcoholism is a critical element in the therapist's campaign to create an intellectually and affectively open
clinical environment. Adult children feel a great deal of active
shame about the areas of dysfunction in their lives, since they
usually see themselves as completely responsible for any pre-
dicaments they are in. Shame reinforces the processes of splitting and repression because the patient must continue to hide
and conceal the self for fear that psychotherapy will expose some
material that will add to an already overflowing reservoir of humiliation. Education about the influence of parental alcoholism
on the development of self-identity, self-esteem, and social and
vocational adjustment is a powerful weapon against shame.
Over time, it helps to diminish paralyzing feelings of failure. As
these feelings do subside, the patient is free to examine the past
and the self more thoroughly.

Education also broadens and deepens experience by reducing
impulsivity. Impulsive actions often follow on the heels of an
intense emotional reaction to some traumatic disappointment
and represent an attempt to discharge the intolerable feelings
associated with such disappointment. This was certainly true in
Paul's case. When I told Paul his sexual behavior was connected
to an intense affect, and that the powerful affect was related

both to current disappointments and important parental (selfobject) failures, several important things happened. Again, his propensity to split off powerful dependency needs was reduced. Also, he was freed from the frightening, and disorganizing, feeling that he was the helpless victim of unpredictable bouts of intense emotionality and destructive behavior. Once the feelings and behavior began to "make sense" in Paul's eyes, his hope of overcoming them was greatly increased, and a measure of control actually gained. As he could refrain from attenuating his emotional reaction to disappointment and isolation by forming a sexual schizoid compromise, the feelings of loneliness intensified, and triggered more memories of childhood frustration, fear, and longing. These new memories helped Paul to accept the fact that many of his problems were, indeed, linked to familial alcoholism. Then, as Paul began to view his behavior as the result of disappointing and destructive interactions with other people, he began to hope that he would behave differently if he was able to form more satisfying relationships. This (and his increasing acceptance of his dependency needs) gave him the courage to open himself to the possibility of new relationships. At the same time, he began to actively disengage from those people in his life who proved consistently disappointing.

It is clear from this example that education is not always, or even often, provided in a discrete, didactic fashion in psychotherapy. It is frequently offered in the context of an interpretation, at a moment when the patient is or has recently been in the throes of an emotional conflict, so that a particular bit of information will likely elucidate the original source of the conflict. As Kohut advised, education is often most useful when it follows immediately upon the therapist's empathic reflection of the patient's emotional state, and serves to explain that state to the patient.

Rita

The nature of Rita's work made her privy to important

financial information about several local businesses. She offered on several occasions to disclose this information to me so that I could profit by making timely investments. When I began to understand the depth of her hopelessness about forming and sustaining rewarding bonds with "normal" people, I reflected to her that she was also afraid that she would not be able to hold my interest and that there would be no lasting bond between us unless I was able to use her to my own advantage in some way. This immediately seemed correct to her, so I went on to explain that she had been accustomed to exploitation by her mother from a very young age. She had eventually come to view exploitation as the only firm base for a relationship. I added that this state of affairs is quite common in alcoholic homes, where parents are often intensely needy and use children to shore up a failing, frightened self.

Principle Number Four: The healing environment must be characterized by recognition and acceptance of the patient's normal need to depend on strong and supportive selfobjects.

The backgrounds of most adult children are marked by a relative dearth of strong, responsive selfobjects capable of mirroring and supporting the evolving self. Therefore, they depend on the therapist for these critical selfobject functions. As the British theorists and Kohut pointed out, this dependency is not at all pathological, but represents a positive development in the therapy. The prognosis for patients improves vastly as they are able to muster the hope and faith that are necessary for a constructive regression to dependency on the therapist.

Dependency needs typically emerge in the context of an unfolding selfobject transference. It is important to remember that British Object Relations theory and Self Psychology view transference in a different way than Freud did. These schools are much more concerned with the repressed and split off aspects of the self, and its relationship to its principal objects and the way in which these are reactivated in the relationship with the therapist, than they are with the breakthrough and displacement of instinctual urges.

Since alcoholic families are so often unreceptive and even hostile to children's expression of their normal needs for mirroring and dependency, these needs are frequently split off from consciousness. Winnicott and Kohut both pointed out that the psychotherapeutic environment, because of its reliability and its intense and exclusive focus on the patient's self, invites regression, or the activation of heretofore concealed, frustrated parts of the self. When these needs are activated in therapy, patients become intensely frightened, and usually redouble their efforts to protect these parts of the self from exposure.

The patient may clearly reveal split off needs for an ideal of strength and calm support (an idealizing selfobject transference).

Paul

Soon after Paul began to experience hopelessness and a sense of impending self-collapse in his sessions with me, he was able to phone me on weekends when these feelings became overwhelming to him. His fright at these times was clear, as was his need for a strong and calming ideal selfobject. It was not necessary for me to offer a solution to his pain, but only to empathize with the loneliness and scariness of his isolation and, once again, to explain that he was reliving a terrifying childhood crisis. I also reassured him that life would not always feel this frightening and futile to him, as his efforts in therapy would eventually lead him out of his awful solitude. These calls seldom lasted longer than five minutes. He seemed to need only this brief contact with an ideal of strength and calmness to tolerate the empty space of the weekend.

It was critical for Paul that I remain "ideal" by not being annoyed, or made anxious by his call. I was never annoyed because he made such obvious efforts to avoid overtaxing me by making his calls so brief. His despair occasionally felt so overwhelming that I urged him (in the manner of his previous therapist) to try to make contact with other people. This was no more helpful to Paul than my warnings of impending disaster were to Ed. It only served to deepen his anxiety and feelings of hopelessness, since any sort of social connectedness was beyond his ability in the early months of our work. He was relying on *me* as a foundation of strength, and when I suggested that he rely on others, I think he felt that I, like his father, was abdicating my responsibilities as a selfobject to soothe and support him in his time of need. I soon realized that if my calls with Paul took longer than five minutes I was trying to do something besides empathize, interpret, and reassure him and I was not responding to the selfobject need.

It should be remembered that transference phenomena can also operate as a resistance in psychotherapy. Freud thought that both positive and negative transference reactions could operate as instruments of resistance. He also described a type of resistance which he called the "negative therapeutic reaction," (Freud [1923] 1962, 39–40). This condition is characterized by a surprising deterioration in a patient's condition just as some progress seems to be taking place in the treatment. Freud noted that some patients seem to want to maintain their neurotic conditions rather than feel better. He related such resistance to the forward progress of the treatment to patients' guilt and masochism.

Kohut saw the negative therapeutic reaction somewhat differently, (1971, 233–235). He believed that a correct interpretation and provision of accurate empathy by the therapist is intensely stimulating to the patient since it suddenly fulfills a profound need that has been frustrated even since childhood. He felt that the patient who suffers from a narcissistic personality disorder lacks the psychic capacity and ego structure necessary to neutralize this excitement and transform it into realistic goals involving relationships, creativity, and work. The unneutralized, untransformed excitement produces the disorganization and panic that are often seen after some pivotal piece of work in the therapy. Kohut observed that, in such cases, the therapy may be blocked until the therapist recognizes the source and meaning of the patient's disturbance.

The negative therapeutic reaction is a formidable source of resistance in psychotherapy, and such reactions are commonly encountered during the course of psychotherapy with adult children of alcoholics. I believe that they are, in the main, transference phenomena. The self of the adult child is usually split between a needy, hurt child, full of longing (equivalent to Fairbairn's "libidinal ego") and a subjectively self-sufficient and other-rejecting pseudo-adult (the antilibidinal ego). The antilibidinal self is the residue of the parents' repeated selfobject failures, and it quite commonly emerges in therapy and reenacts, toward the therapist, its relation to the bad objects of childhood. It defends against the efforts of the libidinal self to regress and establish a dependent relation (selfobject transference) to the therapist. The antilibidinal self experiences the therapist as a "bad" object—potentially disappointing, abusive, exploitative, or rejecting. It will struggle mightily against the frightening prospect of a regression to dependency on such an object. Its resistance typically takes the form of an active withdrawal from the therapist. Such withdrawals may be accompanied by states of disorganization, agitation, rage, and panic, or by an attitude of hopelessness.

The distinguishing feature of a withdrawal is the retreat from an attitude of cooperative self-exploration with the therapist. The withdrawal may be provoked by a therapeutic "error" that summons up images and affects associated with the traumatically disappointing parents. On the other hand, it may also be provoked by a correct interpretation that is accompanied by the therapist's demonstration of her empathic grasp and acceptance of the patient's fundamental, unanswered neediness and long-ing. At such moments of closeness between the patient and ther-apist, the libidinal self longs to surrender the split-off dependency needs to the therapist, and the antilibidinal self must redouble its efforts to maintain these needs in an uncon-scious state. Depending on the relative strength of the antili-bidinal self, the patient may experience a state of agitated conflict, or feelings of paralysis and hopelessness. As the British theorists noted, withdrawals, properly handled by the therapist, can be transformed into clinically desirable regressions to dependence.

Rita

Like Paul, Rita frequently phoned me between sessions in order to obtain the reassurance she needed in order to weather periods of crisis in her life. And, like Paul, she was usually able to gain sufficient reassurance during a phone conversation of about five minutes' duration. However, she could be devastated if I was unable to take her call or to return it within a couple of hours. If I was not quickly available to calm her when she felt terrible, she would usually retaliate by cancelling the next one or two sessions with me. As I learned more about Rita's childhood, and her father in particular, the basis for this strong reaction be-came clear.

When I originally asked about her father and her feelings about him, Rita replied, "My father is a nothing and a nobody. I really don't have anything to say about him. He's just . . . not much of a person." She insisted for a long time that she had no vivid childhood memories of her father.

It was some time before Rita revealed the full extent of her mother's abusiveness. When she finally acknowledged that she had been brutally beaten by her mother through-out her childhood, I asked Rita if her father had ever wit-nessed these beatings, and what he had done about them. Rita remembered that her father had been present for many of the beatings and had done nothing at all about them. In fact, Rita remembered, he turned on his heel and walked out of the room when they were taking place. It was evident to me that when Rita described her father as a "nothing," she really meant that he had been of no use whatsoever to her in the terrible struggle of her childhood. I surmised that when I was unavailable to her during a crisis, it triggered, as Fairbairn would say, "a traumatic release" of the repressed "bad" relationship with her abandoning father. In the timelessness of the unconscious, I *was* her abandoning, completely useless father, and she *was* the desperate child, left to handle a monstrous reality all by herself. In this context, her defensive withdrawal from the prospect of future pain is quite understandable. Further, by canceling her appointments at the last minute Rita was able to relegate me to the role of bereft and hapless victim and discharge into me the feelings of abandonment and disappointment that she needed so desperately to dispel.

I eventually told Rita that I understood that even my temporary unavailability to her was intensely frightening, and that, at such times, it seemed to her as though I was completely useless, and that, moreover, I was an irresponsible, uncaring abandoner who would never be of any help to her. When she was seized by this kind of fear, she had no memory of the many successful efforts I had made to support, understand, and assist her in times of crisis. I was *only* an abandoner; I was, in fact, the incarnation of abandonment. As such, I was a real threat to her psychic survival, and she was bound to muster all available energy for a massive counterassault. Rita immediately recognized the truth of this characterization of her inner state. "It's true," she said, "You become the abandonment. Nothing else." I suggested to her that my unavailability to her when she was in great pain evoked an intense affective memory of her father's dereliction. She was, in effect, reliving the terrible moment when her father turned away and left her to suffer another brutal beating at her mother's hands. This interpretation helped Rita to manage her disappointment in me in a more constructive way. She was gradually able to discuss such feelings about me when they were provoked, and to avoid acting upon them in ways that grossly interfered with our work.

Jack

Though Jack was generally able to recall and describe to me events in his life that had emotional significance for him, he was dismayed by his inability to feel anything at all about these events as he sat with me. There were some important exceptions to this rule, however. On one occasion, he cried during the session when he remembered the fear he felt as a child when he realized he had done something to provoke his father's wrath. He remembered hiding from his father in his tree, or under the table. When I remarked that he must have felt terribly small, alone, and frightened at these times, Jack wrapped his arms around himself, raised his knees to his chest and began to cry and rock on my sofa.

I felt buoyed by the emergence, during the hour, of the hurt and frightened child that Jack's "false" heroic self served to conceal so effectively in every part of his life. This, I said to myself, was a sign of real progress in our relationship. However, during the next session, Jack commented worriedly on our disturbing *lack* of progress. He was sure it was his own fault, he said. He felt "like a slug"— slow and stupid and unable to introduce anything of real importance in therapy. He wondered about my other patients but was reasonably certain that he was the "worst."

"You must want to hit me," he said, and then wished aloud that I would hit him and "get it over with." He reported that he had dreamed of being beaten by me.

I was struck by the temporal connection between his emotional "breakdown" with me and his feelings of doubt and shame and fear about our work together. I pointed it out to Jack, and asked whether these feelings were, in fact, reactions to the exposure of parts of himself that he had many grave doubts about. At this point, Jack described feelings of struggle and conflict that he was beginning to experience in between our sessions, as he realized that he had begun to look forward to seeing me.

"I don't like that," he said. "I tell myself, 'You fool. You should know better.' "

Jack's feelings of doubt about our relationship represented the transferential emergence of the antilibidinal ego and its relation to the "bad" rejecting parts of Jack's parents. This childhood object relationship was activated by the triumph of the libidinal self as it momentarily made good on its longing to reveal itself and be "held" by me. The antilibidinal self was struggling to reassert its control, since it feared I was another "bad" object who, like Jack's parents, would punish Jack for his vulnerability and need. I made this observation to Jack by noting that he had held and rocked himself the previous week, but may have been aware of a wish to be held and soothed by me. I said that I imagined that this wish frightened him a great deal, given his parents' inability to tolerate this kind of longing for comfort, support, and love.

Jack and I traversed this particular stretch of psychic territory many times in our work together. This was to be expected, since it touched at the very heart of his struggle with himself, and the world of objects he longed to join, but who, he believed, could never accept and love the "real" Jack. In the third year of our work together, Jack was able, for the first time, to feel and acknowledge sadness and anxiety about the prospect of my impending month-long vacation. He also had a dream at this time, in which he became aware of a wish to contact me during my absence. In the dream, he tried to phone me for help—something he had never done in reality. When he dialed my number, someone answered and informed him that I'd had to take a month's vacation to escape from his excessive phone calls. As he stood there with the phone to his ear, another Jack came up behind him, and voiced the familiar reproach, "You fool! I told you to stop needing her." However, he was also aware that yet a third Jack was hovering overhead and watching this scenario unfold. This Jack felt reasonably comfortable about making the call, and was not upset by the second Jack's rebuke.

It was always necessary, with Jack, to acknowledge the validity of the claims staked by both the libidinal *and* the antilibidinal self. This acceptance eventually reduced the credibility of the antilibidinal self when it experienced me as a cruel depriver and tormenter. Over time, Jack gained immensely in his ability to override the fears of the antilibidinal self and to gradually shed the false "superkid" self that was its representative in the world of objects.

Principle Number Five: The healing environment must be characterized by an acceptance of individual rights, including the patient's right to protect the self against a well-intentioned therapist.

Many alcoholic parents and enabling spouses exploit children by allowing them to take on roles and tasks that exceed their capabilities and by requiring them to consistently conform to parental need. The psychotherapist who treats adult children usually finds that a great many hours are devoted to helping patients escape their enslavement to a preoccupation with the needs of others. The uncovering and analysis of this preoccupation is an obvious means to this end, but it is not the only one. The therapist must also consistently demonstrate a regard for the patient's right to self-determination by remaining rigorously respectful of the patient's psychological and personal boundaries and by allowing the patient reasonable freedom to determine the course and pace of the psychotherapy. For example, while it is certainly necessary to identify instances of mistrust and defensiveness on the part of the patient, it is also necessary to convey an understanding and acceptance of the roots of such feelings and behaviors, and to refrain from an intensive assault on psychic fortifications as their nature becomes clear. This principle must be observed even when a patient's defensiveness is turned against the well-intentioned, hard-working therapist. In order to construct a healing environment that is respectful of patient rights, the therapist must:
 Examine the destructiveness of the patient's important objects,

as this is tolerable for the patient, and provide explicit support for resisting abusiveness and neglect.

As the alliance with a therapist grows stronger over time, the split-off libidinal self begins to show itself to the therapist. The core of the libidinal self is usually a hurt child, filled with frustrated longing. This hurt child, whom the patient is reluctant to expose to others in his world, is aware of the pain that is aroused in relationships with exploitative and abusive family members, lovers, and friends. When a patient begins to reveal this pain, the therapist can take advantage of the opportunity to explore the toxic nature of particular relationships. As Woititz (1983) observed, adult children who have spent most of their lives in abusive, neglectful, and exploitative environments frequently fail to recognize that the treatment they are receiving from relatives, friends, and lovers is abnormal, destructive, and unacceptable. The therapist must often assist the patient in making these sorts of distinctions by identifying the bad behavior of others when it occurs and commenting on the pain and damage that it causes the patient. The therapist should always support the patient's effort to resist exploitation and abuse by parents or anyone else. (Sometimes the patient can only resist in waking fantasies or in dreams. These efforts should also be recognized and applauded.) The therapist can offer this sort of support to patients by giving them "permission" to resist bad behavior by others, and by reflecting the guilt that they usually feel when they refuse to gratify unreasonable demands by others.

Rita

Rita was accustomed to accept enormous abuse and exploitation from her mother and her (usually alcoholic) lovers. It was surprising to her when I first labeled her mother's public outbursts at her as abusive. It was also several months before she would fully accept my judgment that her married lover was exploiting her by failing to make a commitment to her. She often asked, "Wouldn't you make these kind of sacrifices for a man you loved?" She saw these "sacrifices" as essentially normal even though her lover's repeated betrayals left her feeling suicidal and led to relapses on two occasions. She said that she would feel worthless if she could not free her lover from his wife.

Over the course of several months, I took several steps to help Rita extricate herself from these abusive relationships. I took advantage of every opportunity to elevate her self-esteem by praising her positive attributes and accomplishments. I also explained to her that her mother's brutality had made it hard for her to distinguish the normal give and take of a romantic relationship from the sort of abuse she was presently suffering at the hands of her lover. I observed that children often try to exercise control over their environments by denying the destructiveness in their parents and seeing themselves as bad and worthless. I pointed out that the principal sources of pain for her (her mother and her lover) were also the only sources of love and tenderness in her life, and that she was terrified of losing everything if she began to resist their miserable behavior. (This brought her to tears, as she remembered the beatings she received from her mother as a child, and their anguished aftermath, as she anxiously awaited her mother's knock on the bedroom door.) Finally, I affirmed the appropriateness of her angry and hurt feelings as they gradually emerged in response to the excesses and betrayals of her mother and her lover.

When the anger and the hurt did begin to surface, they frightened Rita very badly. I acknowledged the scariness of finally admitting that the badness was *outside*, and of resisting it and possibly alienating the only people with whom she felt any real connection. However, I also affirmed that she was being treated very badly, and that the abuse was crushing her spirit. I encouraged Rita to focus on her feelings of anger and disappointment as she was able, and, in this way, to gradually increase her tolerance for such feelings (and the experience of outer badness). As Rita did this, she began to have dreams in which she coldbloodedly murdered certain faceless women.

Around the time that Rita began to dream of committing

murder, her mother again humiliated her in front of her co-workers and a friend who was visiting Rita at the office. This time, Rita retaliated by grabbing an expensive clock from her mother's desk and smashing it against the wall. She was so frightened by this incident that she temporarily withdrew from therapy. Yet she was also reassured by the fact that she had smashed the clock instead of her mother, and when her older brother criticized her for her "violent" behavior, she defended herself by pointing to her mother's terrible treatment of her. This was the first time she had been able to feel justifiably angry with her mother, and shortly after this episode she was able to return to school and to perform well in her classes. She also separated from her married lover, and became more assertive with her mother about her financial needs and her wish to be treated respectfully at the office. Rita's struggle with "bad" objects did not end at this point, but it was clear that she had released some of her internal "badness." While there were many periods of anxiety, and extreme sadness after this, she never again spoke of feeling worthless or hopeless.

The patients' reaction to a therapist's effort to support active resistance to exploitation and abuse should determine how far such interventions are carried. It will be recalled that children who have been mistreated cope with intolerable levels of "badness" in their parents by taking the badness into themselves and making it a part of their self-structure so that they feel in control of it. They are extremely fearful of letting these internalized bad objects loose, and filling their worlds with terrifying "devils" once more. They are also fearful of being left alone if they abandon these archaic object relationships. The intensity of the fear experienced is in proportion to the amount of abuse the individual has suffered. Internalized bad objects are always released slowly, however, and the adult child must tolerate enormous anxiety in order to begin to view "badness" as something that may be external to the self. The therapist cannot force this process, but may only give small pushes and reassure the patient by being a "good" (supportive, clam, strong) selfobject. When therapists demand that their patients quickly abandon their ties with destructive objects, they run the risk of repeating a crucial parental error. They may be asking patients to perform beyond their present limits. People who have spent their lives responding only to the needs of others cannot surrender their false selves overnight. The therapist who gives in to disappointment and anger over a patient's "masochism" will probably be placing one more outrageous request in the overwhelmed patient's lap. Adult child patients are typically terribly disappointed in themselves when they give in to exploitation and abuse. I try to ease their minds on such occasions by noting that the need to support and care for others can be a compulsion, just as alcoholism is a compulsion. Alcoholics are prone to relapse even during the course of a good recovery. Children of alcoholics should expect that they will also relapse, even when they are making good progress toward their own recovery.

Therapists often wonder how to proceed when a "bad" object relationship seems to threaten the patient's very survival. Active intervention may be necessary in some cases—say, when the patient becomes actively suicidal or dangerously aggressive. However, psychotherapists who themselves come from alcoholic homes may at times overestimate the extent of the danger that a patient actually faces. This problem is discussed in chapter 7. Especially during the early stages of treatment, adult children are often entangled in so many bad object relationships that their lives are really nothing more than a series of desperate crises. When these terrible relationships provoke a sharp increase in internal conflict and suffering, or produce a sudden rise in active masochism or sadism, it can be very disturbing to the therapist.

Patients may call the therapist with thoughts of suicide or criminal activity, or after relapsing, with psychoactive drugs. Some have called me in the midst of an abusive episode with a spouse. Such events are often best understood as instances of traumatic release, or threatened release, of internalized bad objects. One aspect of the self is rising to defend against powerful demons on the outside. As noted above, a patient's condition may also worsen when split-off need states are suddenly exposed. In either case, the therapist probably gains most by avoiding the role of active combatant in the patient's psychic struggle. While an *offer* to intervene (to arrange an emergency appointment, for example, or call a trusted friend or meet with a spouse) may be welcomed by the patient and serve to calm him, a *threat* to intervene may provoke further deterioration. This is because the patient, in an agitated and disoriented state, hears only the disapproval and disappointment that is contained in the therapist's threat, and not the wish to protect the patient (See the case of Ed, under Principle Two). Thus, the therapist becomes another bad object with whom the patient must struggle.

There are obviously occasions when the therapist must take charge, but it is usually best if one can maintain a supportive, and eventually an interpretive, stance with the patient. I have found it most helpful in these situations to remind patients that they are feeling terrible (and perhaps behaving terribly as well), because they are being used, or abused, or neglected, in ways that remind them of their childhood homes—and which fill them with the same feelings of hopelessness, worthlessness, and dread that they felt as children. I remind them that they are capable of feeling something else, and *being* something else when they are treated with respect and care. I offer them my belief that they will eventually find people who are able to respond to them with kindness and love.

Accept defensiveness. A patient may become defensive toward the therapist if the therapist makes an error, or because of intense need states that patients experience and which threaten to jolt them out of their "inner citadels" (see Principle Four). Defensiveness is always expressed by means of a withdrawal from the active effort to cooperate in the work of the therapy. This withdrawal may take a variety of different forms, such as the emergence of a false heroic, or antisocial self, or an active engagement with destructive objects outside of therapy. However, it always represents the activation of a "bad" object relationship from the patient's childhood, and hence is always transferential in nature. The therapist must be able to tolerate and, eventually, understand defensive maneuvers so that they may be calmly explained to the patient. Then, as the British Object Relations theorists counseled, the patient's withdrawals can become the basis for constructive regressions.

Often, patients withdraw into an old, bad, object relationship immediately upon entering psychotherapy. Paul ended his first session by taking out his checkbook and explaining that he would like to pay me after each session. "I like to keep up to date on all my bills," he said. He started to write the check, but before completing it, looked up once and stared at me for a moment with raised eyebrows. Then he returned to his task. As Paul tore the check from his book and handed it to me, I told him that he had seemed troubled by something as he wrote it, and asked him what he had been thinking and feeling when he looked up at me. "I was thinking that I'll probably end up paying you a lot of money before this is over," he replied. "And I thought maybe you're just going to rip me off." He quickly apologized for this heretical thought. Actually, it seemed a logical enough fear for someone who had been let down as many times as Paul had. I told him that it was natural for him to be afraid and to wonder if I would be like all the other people who had neglected and hurt him.

A colleague saw one patient for a month before he disclosed that he was also being treated by another therapist. He had initiated both treatments at the same time, as a hedge against being left empty-handed should one therapist prove disappointing. This patient had been essentially abandoned by his alcoholic father, who divorced the patient's mother, remarried, and subsequently lavished all his attention on his stepchildren. The patient remembered feeling particularly devastated on the occasion of a rare visit to his father's new home, when he saw his father teach one of the stepsons a card game that the patient and his father had often played together on rainy weekends. My colleague pointed out to the patient that he had been terribly hurt by his father's behavior, and that, even if he had to use his dad's strategy to avoid further pain, he was determined never to be left high and dry again. This colleague did not press her patient for an immediate decision, but suggested to him that he would win a great victory over his past by eschewing his father's solution and making a commitment to one therapist or the other. In this way, he could begin to build the kind of solid connections with people that would provide the final answer to his gnawing anxiety about loss.

One patient's split-off relationship with internalized shaming objects was activated immediately upon his initiation of psychotherapy, and preoccupied him almost constantly during the early months of our work together.

Mike

Mike was the embodiment of the family mascot. The third child of an alcoholic father, he was reared by his parents and his siblings to be the charming and happy baby of the family, a happy distraction from the shame, fear, conflict, and disappointment that his father's drinking produced. Mike remained very faithful to this role until he was fifteen years old, then, his father was killed in an alcohol-related car crash and Mike began to experience periods of mild depression, during which he shed the role of the carefree child. He would express feelings of anxiety about the family's future and recurrent feelings of sadness and regret about his father's death and the way alcohol had robbed him of his father years before it actually killed him. When Mike talked this way, he was told by his mother, or his older sisters, that he was a hypersensitive crybaby who always made mountains out of molehills.

Mike entered therapy at age 30, after a friend observed

that his chronically depressed mood seemed to be preventing him from initiating relationships with women and taking the necessary steps to advance in his career. Mike's friend began taking him to Al-Anon at about the same time that he began to see me. During the first year of our work, Mike's effort to share his memories of and reactions to his father's drinking was disrupted again and again as he was overcome by the feeling that that he was wasting time in Al-Anon and wasting time *and* money in therapy. He repeatedly expressed the fear that he was actually a reasonably well-adjusted person who simply worried and thought too much about himself, and who only felt "sick" because everyone was telling him that adult children of alcoholics are always "sick."[1] He could not shake the feeling that his family was right—that his lingering sadness reflected an immaturity of character and that he was only giving into this babyish part of himself by exploring his "negative" feelings with me or with friends in Al-Anon. He added that delving into these feelings also seemed to deepen his depression, and that he feared that therapy was making him worse instead of better. He frequently spoke of wanting to leave therapy (and to move in with his mother, whom he visited weekly) but also said that he felt that this impulse came from some frightened part of himself.

Throughout that first year Mike's wish to share his grief and fear with me—and to be comforted and helped by me—warred constantly with the powerful and deeply threatened antilibidinal self. In this regard, he was very much like Jack, and very much like many other adult children. The antilibidinal self, of course, wanted to isolate him in order to protect him from the possibility of any more bad object ties. It spoke with his mother's voice, and that of his sisters, and warned him not to be a whiney baby. Mike was also afraid that therapy would deprive him of the bad object ties that represented his only truly significant emotional bonds.

Naturally, it was difficult to hear that Mike's pain was increasing, and that he took so little comfort from our relationship. However, I felt that, given the strength of his family's effort to suppress Mike's emotionality, his antilibidinal self was bound to be a formidable opponent of our work, and thus, the sort of fright that Mike felt was part and parcel of any effort to uncover the hurt child within. Further, it was clear that I could not comfort him very well until his fear quieted somewhat and he could take his eyes off the door long enough to make a real commitment to our work. I never felt impatient with the mercurial quality of Mike's attachment to me. He was quite impatient with himself, however, and often berated himself for his inability to settle down and "do the work" that would help him. To join in this attack would only have made me another bad object who threatened the integrity of Mike's self. Instead I observed that his struggles with his family around emotional sharing made his present struggle with himself quite understandable. I observed that alcoholic families frequently convey a powerful message to children that their needs for intimacy, support, and comfort are pathological, and I reassured him that, in fact, these feelings were a very human, and very valuable, part of him. I also applauded the courage he displayed in standing up to the part of himself that wished to annihilate his needs, and remaining in therapy.

Mike's active struggle with his antilibidinal self diminished greatly early in the second year of our work. He began to joke about his wish to leave therapy and to move in with his mother. He visited his mother less frequently, and he began to recover and report important memories of his father's drinking, and to explore the emotional impact of these events with me.

While Mike was able to settle into our work within a year's time, other patients may find it necessary (as Rita did on more than one occasion) to take a leave of absence from psychotherapy. I believe that the therapist should help the patient to understand a compelling need to leave the therapy, but should not strongly oppose it. It is usually more important to respect a patient's right to protect the threatened core of the self and to direct the course of her life than it is to continue the therapy at the moment. Comings and goings of this sort can actually be seen as a part of the process of psychotherapy.

Defensiveness may take many forms. Some attempts to withdraw from the relationship are fairly transparent, while others are subtle and difficult to detect.

Jack

During one lengthy period of my work with Jack, I found that I often became unbearably sleepy during our sessions. I tried to link these recurrent episodes with either the content of Jack's associations or some other aspect of our interaction with one another, but I was unable to develop any compelling hypothesis.

One day, Jack began the hour by describing his reactions to the previous session. It had been a particularly intense session during which he had talked, and cried a little about, the feelings of deprivation from his childhood. Jack said that after this session, he felt very drained. He drove home, walked out to the wooded area behind his house and sat down on a log and tried to think over the things we discussed that day. As he sat in the woods, and thought about the session, he became terribly sleepy.

I had begun to feel sleepy as soon as Jack started to talk, but this description of his experience with sudden intense fatigue jolted me to full consciousness. I asked if he had ever felt this way during our sessions, and he replied, "Oh yes, all the time." I asked him to describe the kinds of thoughts and feelings that occurred to him when this sleepiness washed over him, and he explained that he often imagined himself being held by his tree at these times— the tree that he had run to as a child, when he was full of fright or hurt or anger that could not be expressed to his parents.

While empathy often occurs on a relatively intellectual plane, therapists may also apprehend a patient's inner state in a very primal way. I actually experienced Jack's need to flee from the possibility of shared emotionality.

Further, I experienced it in much the same way that he experienced it, as a painful, yet very nearly irresistible urge to withdraw from consciousness. I explained to Jack that he was afraid of feeling deeply in my presence, since his parents had punished, or ignored signs of emotional vulnerability in him, and there was some possibility that I would behave in the same way. Therefore, he *had* to remove himself from me when he was full of feeling. Logically enough, he escaped to the only reliable source of comfort that he had ever known, the strong and loving old tree that grew in the backyard of his childhood home. Jack was, as always, embarrassed by his retreat from me, but I continued to emphasize that this was a natural response to past hurts and disappointments.

Jack was frequently tempted to flee to his tree during the course of our work together. Once we understood that this was happening, however, he was usually able to avoid a full scale withdrawal. Instead, he would say, "I want to go to the tree right now." This was my cue to concentrate on the character of his immediate emotional state, so that I could share in it, and so that he might be held by my empathic understanding, and be supported, for once, by a fully human selfobject.

The adult child's turn to new object relationships is always gradual. Portions of the self are slowly withdrawn from the bad object relationships and slowly "handed over" to the therapist. The therapist cannot force this process. Imploring or commanding patients to change only re-creates the traumatic pressure to exceed one's limits that is characteristic of the alcoholic home. As adult children progress through psychotherapy, they necessarily fluctuate between states of withdrawal, constructive regression, and actively expressed need for the therapist. Therefore, the therapist must alternately affirm patients' rights to expect normal amounts of warmth and caring, and the legitimacy of their needs to retreat, at times, from those who seem to offer it.

Summary

Psychotherapy heals and strengthens the self of the adult child insofar as it redresses the important failings of the alcoholic home. When the therapist provides a stable, emotionally responsive, and emotionally open environment for these patients, they are gradually able to reveal their repressed and split-off needs for calm, strong, mirroring selfobjects. However, the initial emergence of these needs badly frightens most adult children who enter therapy, and they unconsciously erect powerful barriers to further exposure of these long-buried parts of the self. Patients' defensiveness may appear as aggressiveness, self-destructiveness or hopelessness," or may involve some form of abandonment of the therapist. These sorts of withdrawal from active cooperation with the therapist may also be provoked by therapist's errors, or by some traumatic disappointment that occurs outside of therapy. In any case, the therapist must be able to tolerate these periods of fragmentation until their meaning can be divined and the selfobject needs at their base can be explained to the adult child. If the selfobject needs remain buried because the therapist cannot tolerate the means used to defend against them, they will retain their power to deplete the self and to maintain active self-loathing.

Note

1. Though Al-Anon does press its members to recognize that they are making "sick" responses to an unhealthy family situation, I believe that this further weakens the adult child's self-esteem, which is already at a critically low level. When adult children tell me their behavior is "sick," I reply that they are doing the things that they needed to do as

children to survive psychologically (and sometimes physically) in an alcoholic home. That is, these behaviors (rescuing, retreating, hiding, and fighting, for example) were adaptive at one time. The very existence of these behaviors, I explain, is a testimony to the patient's strength and ability to defend himself. I also explain that now that the patient is grown and out of the parental home, the behavior must change so that new, more constructive and rewarding relationships can be built with partners who are not actively alcoholic. The process of change is necessarily slow and painful. Like the evolution of the self in recovery from alcoholism, the change and growth of the self in adult children is a process, not an event.

7

WHEN THE FAMILY HERO
TURNS PRO:
THE ADULT CHILD
IN THE
HELPING PROFESSIONS

M ANY CHILDREN from alcoholic homes sacrifice a substantial portion of their selfhood in order to minister to the physical and psychic needs of their parents, or parent-surrogates. They are moved to this sacrifice by love and compassion for their parents, by their fear of losing their parents, and by their longing for a satisfying, sustaining self-selfobject relation (see chapter 4). They also greatly prefer the role of a strong helper to that of a dependent, fearful child. Vulnerable aspects of the self are therefore split off, and most of the time are unavailable to conscious awareness. Some of these children, when they are grown, extend their largess to the wider community by entering the helping professions. A sizable number of these instinctive helpers choose to specialize in the treatment of chemically dependent individuals and families. They often bring to their work an extraordinary capacity for empathy, and their will to restore the suffering alcoholics and their codependents can become the basis for the very qualities of hope, courage, and dogged perseverance that are indispensable to success in this field. However, in the adult child whose heroic role armor has not been pierced by self-analysis, supervision, or psychotherapy, this will to restore usually operates as a compulsive, destructive force. Fueled, in large measure, by fear and flagging self-esteem, it may actually interfere with the process of recovery.

The Heroic Therapist's Will to Restore: Clinical Ramifications

The hero, once again, is the unfailingly "good" child in the alcoholic family, who, like Jack, accepts the standard of responsibility when it falls from the hands of the drinking parent and the enabling spouse. As the disease of alcoholism progresses, and the family situation deteriorates, the hero's burden of responsibility and fear increases, and the unconscious longing for a healthful, supportive self–selfobject relation intensifies. Eventually the hero's possibilities for transcending the narrowly defined familial role of selfless helper are seriously eroded. This child often becomes as compulsively devoted to the restoration of the family as the alcoholic is devoted to the pursuit and use of alcohol.

If the will to restore is an important guiding principle in the life of the hero, it will doubtless emerge as crucial to the attitudes and approaches that the heroic therapist brings to his professional functions. It is likely to be repeatedly evoked in those situations in which the therapist's work requires daily confrontations with the disease of alcoholism, and it should be especially powerful where the therapist's own life as a hero remains essentially unexamined and the need to restore is unrecognized, and thus beyond conscious control. The clinical phenomenon most commonly associated with the will to restore is an impatient "rush to recovery" by the therapist. The therapist whose self-esteem and sense of emotional safety depends on the patient's restoration to wholeness is often intolerant of the lengthy and inevitable periods of withdrawal, fragmentation, and regression that precede recovery, and will often attempt to abbreviate or evade these painful phases. Heroic therapists are particularly apt to block patients' expressions of hopelessness, panic, and rage, since they associate such feelings with the possibility of loss or agonizing conflict with the object. They know, from experience with their own parents, that these intense affects usually signal real trouble in that they may lead to physical abusiveness, relapse, or other destructive behaviors. It is most important to understand that, in the heroic therapist's family of origin, emotionality and conflict never came to a good end. When these therapists move to prevent an explosion of feeling in a psychotherapy session, they are recapitulating a scene from childhood in which an understandable attempt was made to fulfill role expectations, to avoid loss and feelings of intense fear and failure, and to curtail parental destructiveness. While the abridgement of emotionality was an adaptive maneuver in childhood, however, it is likely to hinder rather than facilitate recovery when it is practiced by a therapist. It should, in fact, be regarded as a member of the broad class of enabling behaviors.

It may be helpful to consider some clinical vignettes that illustrate the unconscious suppression of explosive affect by a clinician and its deleterious effects on the course of therapy with chemically dependent and codependent clients. The first vignette describes my own painful experience with a highly self-destructive narcotics addict; the second details a blockage in the work of a supervisee who was treating a suicidally depressed adult child.

Jeremy

Jeremy was a 27-year-old man who had been addicted to prescription narcotics since the age of 18. The onset of his addiction was associated with his release from a state mental hospital, where he had been a patient since the age of 16. Prior to his commitment, Jeremy had spent two years in a private psychiatric hospital. He was transferred to the state facility when his parents' insurance benefits were exhausted.

Though Jeremy was a frequent runaway prior to age 14, there seems to have been no very good psychiatric reason for his institutionalization. He was a highly intelligent and resourceful youngster running from a sexually abusive father and an intensely envious, rageful mother who held him up to constant ridicule and humiliation. His parents made the decision to hospitalize him when they decided to separate. In retrospect, it seems as though they may have been scapegoating him for the failure of the family as well as seeking an alternative, low-cost solution to the problem of child care and supervision. (Jeremy's younger sister was sent away to private school at the same time.)

Jeremy's mother visited him once during the four years of his hospitalization; his father never visited him at all. Abandoned to, and suddenly dependent upon, the care of strangers, Jeremy was at first disconsolate. He cried much of the first week. Afterward, however, he made a conscious decision to steel himself to all present and future terrors. He told himself, "I will not cry, and I will not be afraid."

This bravado served him well in the hospital environment, where his outrageous pranks relieved the tedium and quiet desperation of his mates. His toughness and ability to endure also enabled him to survive racial harassment and violence in the state hospital and to successfully resist a mistaken attempt to subject him to electroconvulsive shock. No lamb to the slaughter he, Jeremy hurled a chair in front of the door to his room when told that he had been scheduled for shock treatment, and began to scream for his doctor. He continued to scream until the doctor arrived and corrected the wrongful order.

Though Jeremy survived the hospitals as well as, if not better than, many others might have, he walked away with a profound inner emptiness and deep sense of worthlessness because of his abandonment by his parents and his feeling that he must have done something to warrant the loss of their love. Heavily tranquilized during his four years of hospitalization, he also walked away with a deep dependency on mood-altering drugs. Jeremy expended enormous effort in his post-hospital life trying to overcome his fundamental distrust of others in order to build a relationship that might answer his sense of emptiness. However, he was helplessly ensnared in the "infinite loop": Each new love proved to be a compulsive abandoner somewhat worse than the last. Jeremy responded to each new experience of disappointment much as he had the first, with a determination not to grieve, and displays of bravado that, over the years, became increasingly antisocial and self-destructive. For example, his dependence on prescription narcotics and his supreme delight at conning physicians into writing prescriptions for him grew into an addiction to Dilaudid and eventually, heroin. Further, he felt compelled to haggle with, challenge, and curse the biggest and most dangerous-looking street-corner dealers. He began to shoplift, and to steal from his employer. The money that he made from these activities was sometimes used for drugs, but more often, given to friends.

Jeremy's most frightening binges of drug abuse, aggression, and thievery would occur after a woman had disappointed him. For this reason, my spirits would plunge when he would initiate one of these hopeless relationships. I would feel my own panic mount as he became increasingly rageful about each betrayal by his new lover, and as he began to consciouly contemplate, during his sessions, the prospect of a binge to relieve his inner turmoil. I deeply feared that Jeremy would be arrested and imprisoned (which I thought might lead him to become suicidal), or that he would be beaten and left for dead by an angry dealer, or that he would overdose or perhaps inject air into his veins (a frequent fantasy when he held a syringe and needle in his hands). My fears were accompanied by feelings of helplessness and self-doubt concerning my ability to assist him.

I usually responded to this complex of emotions with a

flurry of activity. Jeremy refused to enter inpatient treatment for his addiction, since he felt that hospitalization would signify a capitualation to his parents' efforts to locate their illness in him. Therefore, when he was in the midst of or on the edge of a binge, I would help him devise plans to remove himself from the immediate source of his unbearable feelings by putting him out of touch with the woman who was troubling him. Jeremy had a very constructive friend who lived some miles out of town. This "good" object was always glad to put Jeremy up for a few weeks, and his obvious caring for Jeremy had a most salutary effect on Jeremy's shattered self-esteem. This friend often lectured Jeremy, making explicit references to his considerable waste of intellect and talent. I would refer Jeremy to his friend when my attempts to interpret his dilemma failed to quiet him. If he refused to effect the "geographic solution" I would usually end up lecturing him myself. This represented a considerable departure from my usual therapeutic attitude, which relies heavily on the restorative powers of empathy and the calm elucidation of inner conflict. When I found myself in the middle of a lecture, I understood that I was in trouble.

Jeremy lived with his mother, and one night, in the middle of a prolonged binge of chemical abuse, and after an extended period of emotional chaos between Jeremy and his latest lover, his mother challenged his self-destructive behavior in a manner that strikingly clarified the dynamic beneath my own ill-fated attempts to save Jeremy from himself and, coincidentally, suggested a rationale for his inability to save himself. At about 2 A.M., Jeremy telephoned a friend and made plans to go downtown with him to purchase some heroin. Jeremy's mother, who had been listening to the call on an extension phone, ran into the living room and begged him not to leave the apartment. They argued, but Jeremy was determined to go.

When logic failed, when threats failed, Jeremy's exasperated mother grabbed a dinette chair and threw it in front of the door. Needless to say, this gesture was also in vain, but in Jeremy's account of his mother's behavior, I heard an echo, not just of my own fears, but of the desperation and panic he had felt in the hospitals, where he too, had once thrown a chair.

I asked if he had felt scared about the plan to buy the heroin, and he replied that he had not. He had only felt angry at his mother for trying to stop him. I then told him that I had felt very frightened by his plans and his behaviors on several occasions, as his mother apparently did, and asked if he had ever felt this kind of deep fear about his own survival. Jeremy became thoughtful and spoke of two occasions which had so terrified him. The first involved an act of sexual abuse by his father, and the second, of course, was the time he had been threatened with shock. He became very upset when speaking of these two incidents; his voice lost its customary tone of anger and defiance and becoming sad and small. I understood, then, the continuing importance and impact of the vow Jeremy had made during his first week in the hospital, when he said, "I will not cry and I will not be afraid." He had banished (split off) his terrible fears and his deep emptiness in the certain knowledge that he could not afford them in the hostile environment of a psychiatric institution, and he was continuing to keep them at bay with the same brand of reckless and counterphobic daredeviltry that he had practiced back then. At the same time, his mother and I, like countless other codependents down through the ages, were caught up in his furious effort to avoid a confrontation with his deepest hurt. We were moved by our abiding, but misguided belief that the experience and expression of painful feelings must always lead to disaster for the ones we love and arouse feelings of shame, failure, and hopelessness in ourselves. So, we protected Jeremy from his true feelings, by experiencing them for him. *We* felt the terror—the sense of impending disaster and irretrievable loss that he was determined not to feel or remember. In our terror, we barred the door and tried to wrestle his compulsion to the mat. In doing so, we became the enemy, and Jeremy was able to take refuge in the anger and defiance that he had determined to substitute for feelings of terror and abandonment.

To alter this unproductive pattern, I had to recognize that in my own desperation to see Jeremy well and free of the awful feelings that fed his compulsion, I was coercing healthful solutions to self-destructive urges. Further, I had to accept that such solutions were temporary at best. At worst, they communicated a fear of the dark feelings that lay beneath these urges rather than the understanding and acceptance that was necessary to assuage these feelings. Further, my panicky maneuverings indicated a lack of faith in Jeremy's ability to tolerate his feelings and work them through. This deepened his sense of isolation and also did further damage to his self-esteem.

I was eventually able to integrate my new understandings into my work with Jeremy. I continued to reflect and to ask about his panic and his sadness. I was able to avoid constructing alternatives to his binge behavior because, as he was able to describe and actually feel his terror of losing control, he was motivated to construct these solutions himself. I should add that this development was a long while in unfolding. He had been deeply opposed to exploring the feelings of panic and loss from the outset of therapy, and strongly resisted my attempt to amplify these themes in our work. However, my victory over my own fear of his pain and my helplessness helped him to accept his emotional vulnerability. When he finally did so he was also able to more fully acknowledge the seriousness of his problem with drugs. He entered an inpatient detoxification program, and then, a rehabilitation center for chemically dependent individuals. He eventually joined Narcotics Anonymous.

I have also seen the will to restore affect the work of many of my consultees and supervisees who are the adult children of alcoholic parents. They, too, often seem compelled to stifle the expression of affect that must emerge in the course of a successful recovery.

David

In one case, an adult child under my supervision treated an extremely depressed and masochistic middle-aged man who was himself the adult child of an alcoholic mother who had died from the complications of her disease. David made three unsuccessful attempts at suicide during his twenties and thirties, and when he entered therapy, was facing a combination of vocational, physical, and familial problems that were rekindling these feelings of desperation. Though he was terrified of intimacy and had been socially isolated for years, David was able to respond to the concern and skilled intervention of my supervisee, and formed a strong bond with her.

As his trust in her increased, he was able to share the depth of his despondency with her, and began to use his sessions to talk about his intense feelings of worthlessness and his wish to die. He also revealed that he had been stockpiling the sedatives that had been prescribed for his insomnia. These revelations represented an investment of profound faith in the therapist and were a mark of real progress in the work. However, the therapist—who had grown up with an alcoholic, depressed mother—was greatly disturbed by her patient's feelings and blocked them at every turn. Abandoning empathy and cooperative exploration, she argued with David as to whether his situation was truly hopeless; and though she had spent countless hours working with him to help him overcome his attitude of masochistic self-sacrifice toward his family, she now began to tell him he must give up the option of suicide in order to ensure their future well-being and happiness.

The therapist was well aware that she had lost the empathic thread at this point, and she knew that she was conveying an attitude of disappointment and disapproval toward her client that served only to heighten his feelings of isolation and failure. She felt compelled to persist in this behavior, however, as if to smother his despair with her hope. Undoubtedly, this was a strategy she had developed in an effort to deal with her own mother. When this therapist brought her dilemma to supervision, I suggested that she fight her patient's depression, not by beating it to death, but by reestablishing the empathic bond and thereby reducing his sense of isolation and rejection. I pointed out that David had good reason to feel terrible, and that it would be meaningful and uplifting to him if she could do what his parents had never been able to do—acknowledge and accept his pain and weather it with him.

Of course, the therapist was well aware that despair must be expressed and shared before it can be resolved, but it was very hard for her to allow this phase of the therapy to unfold. Her compulsive will to restore her client to a state of balance and ease played havoc with her usually excellent clinical judgement and execution.

Summary

The British theorists, and Kohut, have taught that psychotherapy should provide a secure, accepting environment in which split-off and at times chaotic and desperate parts of the self are free to reveal themselves. These regressions represent a necessary emotional surrender to the therapist for holding and soothing, and they are an important aspect of the healing process. This is especially true where emotional deprivation has been severe and the psyche is pervasively split. The task of the therapist is to respond to the needy and desperate parts of the self in such a way as to correct original parental failures.

The alcoholic parent and the enabling spouse have typically failed their children in many ways. However, their inability to tolerate, let alone accept and understand, their children's suffering is usually a key failure. Many children of alcoholics are raised in a condition of constant threat, and are subject to intense and disturbing affects of every variety. They are forced, however, to split off their panic, and their overwhelming sadness, and their feelings of humiliation and despair must be disposed of in similar fashion. This is because alcoholic parents, and their alcohol-preoccupied partners, are engaged in a des-

perate struggle with demons of their own, and have little time
or inclination to listen to their children's pain. They simply do
not have the psychic resources to soothe a child, or to say "Tell
me about it," and to work toward a resolution of frightening
feelings. Children of alcoholics understand that they cannot
manage their intense feelings by themselves, and they become
frightened of the emotionally turbulent and needy parts of themselves, which they consign to the unconscious. Adult children of
alcoholics also learn to equate emotionality with the onset of
destructive behavior in their parents, and this tends to reinforce
the unconscious resolution to avoid intense feeling.

Thus, many children of alcoholics enter adulthood estranged
from their own emotional reality, and hopeless as to the potential of human relationships to soothe and strengthen the self.
Therapists who seek to correct these deficits must be relatively
free of such problems themselves. Indeed, they must be able to
stimulate, as well as tolerate, the reemergence of split-off and
intensely distressed aspects of a patient's self. These reemerge
as the therapeutic alliance develops, and the heroic therapist,
with a deep commitment to the recovery of dependent and co-
dependent clients, and with a profound understanding of the
nature of their struggle, may easily inspire the confidence that
is necessary to strengthen this alliance. The heroic therapist
may falter, however, as the alliance bears fruit and the patient
begins to experience, and attempts to share, these parts of the
self that have been hidden and feared since early childhood.
The therapist, like the patient, may fear the destructive potential of intense emotion, and may abhor the arousal and expression of deep emotional need in others that can awaken the
hidden longings of the self. If so, then she is likely to hinder
recovery by employing obstructive maneuvers that she once
used to restore the false harmony of the alcoholic family and
of the self.

The real goal of psychotherapy is not to eliminate painful
affect, or eradicate patients' dependency needs, but to foster a

sense of psychic integrity and hope. This is accomplished when frightened, lonely parts of the patient's self are allowed to become conscious, and accessible to the soothing, strengthening, and moderating influence of healthful human relationships.

REFERENCES

Black, C. 1981. *It Will Never Happen to Me!* Denver: M. A. C.

Fairbairn, W. R. D. [1940] 1981. "Schizoid Factors in the Personality." In Fairbairn, *Psychoanalytic Studies of the Personality.*

Fairbairn, W. R. D. [1943] 1981. "The Repression and the Return of Bad Objects." In Fairbairn, *Psychoanalytic Studies of the Personality.*

Fairbairn, W. R. D. [1944] 1981. "Endopsychic Structure Considered in Terms of Object-Relationships." In Fairbairn, *Psychoanalytic Studies of the Personality.*

Fairbairn, W. R. D. 1981. *Psychoanalytic Studies of the Personality.* 7th ed. London: Routledge and Kegan Paul.

Freud, S. 1932. *New Introductory Lectures on Psychoanalysis.* London: Hogarth Press.

Freud, S. [1912] 1959. *The Dynamics of the Transference.* (Vol. 2 of the Collected Papers.)

Freud, S. [1915] 1959. *Instincts and Their Vicissitudes* (Vol. 4 of the Collected Papers.)

Freud, S. [1917] 1959. *Mourning and Melancholia.* (Vol. 4 of the Collected Papers.)

Freud, S. [1923] 1962. *The Ego and the Id.* New York: Norton.

Freud, S. 1959. *Collected Papers*, vols. 2, 4. New York: Basic Books.

Gravitz, H. L. and J. D. Bowden. 1985. *Guide to Recovery: A Book for Adult Children of Alcoholics*. Holmes Beach, Fla.: Learning Pubs.

Grotstein, J. S. 1982. "Newer Perspectives in Object Relations Theory." *Contemporary Psychoanalysis*, vol. 18, no. 1.

Guntrip, H. 1969. *Schizoid Phenomena, Object Relations and the Self*. 7th ed. New York: International Universities Press.

Heimann, P. [1952] 1983. "Certain Functions of Introjection and Projection in Early Infancy." In M. E. Klein, et al., eds. *Developments in Psychoanalysis*.

Jacobson, E. 1954. "Contribution to the Metapsychology of Psychotic Identification." *Journal of the American Psychoanalytic Association* 2:239–262.

Jacobson, E. 1964. *The Self and the Object World*. New York: International Universities Press.

Jacobson, E. 1967. *Psychotic Conflict and Reality*. New York: International Universities Press.

Klein, M. E. [1946] 1983. "Notes on Some Schizoid Mechanisms." In Klein, et al., eds. *Developments in Psychoanalysis*.

Klein, M. E., P. Heimann, S. Isaacs, and J. Riviere, eds. 1952. *Developments in Psychoanalysis*. London: Hogarth, Reprint: New York: Da Capo Press, 1983.

Kohut, H. 1971. *The Analysis of the Self*. New York: International Universities Press.

Kohut, H. 1977. *The Restoration of the Self*. New York: International Universities Press.

Kohut, H. 1984. *How Does Analysis Cure?* Chicago: University of Chicago Press.

Kohut, H. and S. Wolf. 1978. "The Disorders of the Self and Their Treatment: An Outline." *International Journal of Psychoanalysis* 59:413–424.

LaPlanche, J. and J.-B. Pontalis. 1973. *The Language of Psychoanalysis*. New York: Norton.

Meissner, W. W. 1984. *The Borderline Spectrum*. New York: Jason Aronson.

Wegscheider, S. 1981. *Another Chance: Hope and Health for the Alcoholic Family*. Palo Alto, Calif.: Science and Behavior Books.

Whitfield, C. 1987. *Healing the Child Within*. Hollywood, Fla.: Health Communications.

Winnicott, D. W. [1948] 1975. "Paediatrics and Psychiatry." In Winnicott, *Through Paediatrics to Psychoanalysis*.

Winnicott, D. W. [1954a] 1975. "Metapsychological and Clinical Aspects of Regression Within the Psycho-Analytical Set-up." In Winnicott, *Through Paediatrics to Psychoanalysis*.

Winnicott, D. W. [1954b] 1975. "Withdrawal and Regression." In Winnicott, *Through Paediatrics to Psychoanalysis*.

Winnicott, D. W. [1955] 1975. "Clinical Varieties of Transference." In Winnicott, *Through Paediatrics to Psychoanalysis*.

Winnicott, D. W. [1956] 1975. "Primary Maternal Preoccupation." In Winnicott, *Through Paediatrics to Psychoanalysis*.

Winnicott, D. W. [1971] 1975. Letter to Mme. Jeannine Kalmanovitch. Excerpt in Masud Khan's Introduction. In Winnicott, *Through Paediatrics to Psychoanalysis*.

Winnicott, D. W. 1975. *Through Paediatrics to Psychoanalysis*. New York: Basic Books.

Woititz, J. 1983. *Adult Children of Alcoholics*. Hollywood, Fla.: Health Communications.

Wurmser, L. 1981. *The Mask of Shame*. Baltimore: Johns Hopkins University Press.

INDEX

Adult children of alcoholics
  alcoholic lifestyle of, x, 12, 42, 65
  and the return of the bad object,
    64–67
  as psychotherapists, xi, 134, 144–
    55
  fear of dependency and attach-
    ment, 62–64
  general characteristics of (*See also*
    Family hero, Family mascot,
    Family scapegoat, and Lost
    child), ix–x, 7, 9–12, 23–24, 38,
    40–41, 51, 55–56, 62, 63, 64, 65,
    67–70, 113, 117, 120, 122, 125,
    130, 141, 144, 154
  infinite loop. *See* Adult children, al-
    coholic lifestyle
  instability of, 62–67
  narcissistic vulnerability of, 58–62
  separation-individuation problems,
    39–58, 52, 58
Al-Anon, 5, 138, 142–43
Alcoholic families
  general characteristics of, x, 1–4,
    10, 41, 42–43, 44, 58, 62–63, 67,
    69, 109–10, 112–13, 117, 122,
    123, 130, 139, 153–54
Alcoholics Anonymous, 5, 39
Anonymous organizations (*See also*
  Al-Anon, Alcoholics Anonymous,
  Narcotics Anonymous), 1, 43

Antilibidinal ego (*See* Ego,
  antilibidinal)

Basic endopsychic situation (*See also*
  Endopsychic structure), 21–23,
  73
Black, Claudia, x, 4, 7, 9, 12, 117
British object relations theorists (*See
  also* Fairbairn, W.R.D., Guntrip,
  H., and Winnicott, D.W., xi, 20–
  30, 37, 41, 43, 71, 72, 74, 98, 99
  on defense and resistance in psy-
    chotherapy, 75
  on early relationships to objects,
    29
  on goals of psychotherapy, 12, 104,
    107
  on internalization of bad objects,
    29
  on patient dependency in psy-
    chotherapy, 122
  on process and technique in psy-
    chotherapy, 87, 104–5, 107
  on regression psychotherapy, 98,
    126
  on repression, 82, 98
  on splitting, 29, 75, 82
  on the therapeutic environment,
    153
  on transference, 82, 86, 98, 122–23

Classical analytic school of object relations, 30–32
Co-Dependence, x, 1, 152–53

Defense-Resistance in psychotherapy. *See* Psychotherapy and psychoanalysis, defense-resistance in

Ed, 48–51, 63–64, 102, 114, 116, 135
Ego, 14, 15, 32, 37, 38, 55, 69, 72, 74, 83, 86
    antilibidinal (*See also* Basic endopsychic situation, Endopsychic structure, and Internal saboteur), 22–23, 28, 59–62, 67, 69, 73, 76, 78, 95, 125, 126, 129, 138, 139
    central (*See also* Basic endopsychic situation, and Endopsychic structure), 21, 22, 37, 60, 64, 67, 68, 73, 76
    development of, 15–16, 17–18
    functions of, 15
    libidinal (*See also* Basic Endopsychic situation and Endopsychic structure), 21–23, 28, 37, 60, 64, 69, 73, 76, 77, 95, 125, 126, 129, 131
    nature of, 31
    reality, 36–37
    regressed, 28, 78
Empathy, 33, 34, 44, 57, 64, 74, 92, 97, 98–101, 102, 103, 105, 107, 121, 124, 125, 140–41, 144
Endopsychic structure (*See also* Antilibidinal ego, Basic endopsychic situation, Central ego, Internal saboteur, and Libidinal ego), 20, 21–23
English school of object relations (*See also* Heimann, P. and Klein, M.), 17–19
Erikson, E., 30

Fairbairn, W. R. D., 12, 20–25, 27, 28, 32, 57, 63, 73, 76–78, 84, 91–92, 93
    on antilibidinal ego, 22–23, 59–60, 73, 76, 78, 125
    on basic endopsychic situation, 21–23, 73
    on central ego, 21–23, 37, 73, 76
    contributions to a psychology of the self, 29–30
    on defense-resistances in psychotherapy, 76–78
    on development of psychic structure, 20–25
    on endopsychic structure, 20–23
    on goals of psychotherapy, 73
    on internationalized bad objects, 21–24, 54–55, 59–60, 64–65, 67, 77–78, 84, 90, 91–92, 99, 126
    on libidinal ego, 21–23, 37, 69, 73, 76, 77, 125
    on mature relation to objects, 24–25
    on nature of instincts, 20, 29
    on negative therapeutic reaction, 77
    on process and technique in psychotherapy, 91–92
    on psychopathology, 21, 22
    on psychotherapists as good objects, 91–92, 97, 103
    on repression, 20, 73, 76, 84
    on schizoid phenomena, 20–23, 62, 91
    on splitting, 73, 90
    on transference, 65, 84
False self, 25–26, 43–51, 62, 68, 73, 76, 83, 87, 89, 128, 130, 134, 136
Family hero, 8, 9, 10, 41, 44, 45–48, 51, 128, 136, 145
Family mascot, 9, 44, 137
Family roles (*See also* Family hero, Family mascot, Family scapegoat, and Lost child), 7–9, 44

Family scapegoat, 8, 9, 11, 44, 48–51, 136
Freud, S., 17, 20, 27, 91
  on defense-resistance in psycho-
    analysis, 74, 124
  on ego development, 15–16
  on functions of ego, 15
  on goals of psychoanalysis, 72
  on internalization of objects, 16
  on nature of the object, 16
  on negative therapeutic reaction, 124
  on process and technique in psy-
    choanalysis, 87
  on psychic topography, 14–16
  on transference, 81–82, 85, 122–23, 124

Giovachini, P., 34
Goals of psychotherapy. *See* Psychotherapy and psychoanalysis,
  goals of
Grotstein, J., 24
  on Fairbairn's contributions, 29–30
Guntrip, H., 12, 20, 27–29, 60, 63,
  73–74, 78–80, 84–85, 92–97, 122–23
  on antilibidinal ego, 95, 78
  on defense-resistance in psycho-
    therapy, 78–80, 93, 95, 98
  on development of psychic struc-
    ture, 27–29
  on goals of psychotherapy, 73–74
  on identification with bad objects, 78
  on internalized bad objects, 93
  on libidinal ego, 28, 95
  on patient dependency needs in
    psychotheraphy, 94–95
  on process and technique in psy-
    chotherapy, 92–97
  on psychotherapists as good ob-
    jects, 92, 93–94, 103
  on regressed ego, 28, 78

on regression in psychotherapy, 78,
  84–85, 92–93, 96
on schizoid phenomena, 27–28, 62,
  73, 78–80, 92–97
on splitting, 28, 78
on stages of psychotherapy, 92–93, 98
on transference, 84–85, 95

Healing environment, 108–42, 153
  acceptance of patient defensiveness
    in, 135–42
  acceptance of patient rights as in-
    dividual in, 130–42
  education in, 120–22
  enlargement of emotional experi-
    ence in, 117–20
  meeting patient selfobject needs in,
    122–30
  necessary qualities of, 108–42, 153
  openness of, 116–22
  stability of, 112–16
  support for resisting abuse, 130–35
  warmth, responsiveness and ac-
    ceptance in, 109–12
Hartmann, H., 30
Heimann, P.
  on development of psychic struc-
    ture, 17–18
  on psychological impact of inner
    objects, 18

Id, 14, 15, 86
Idealization, 34, 35, 74, 95, 102, 123
Identification, 16, 38, 55, 67, 68, 78
Incorporation, 54
Infinite loop (*See* Adult children, al-
  coholic lifestyle of)
Internal saboteur (*See also* Antilibidi-
  nal ego), 22, 59–62, 63
Internalized bad objects (*See also*
  Antilibidinal ego, Basic endo-
  psychic situation, Libidinal ego),

21, 21–24, 29, 38, 51–58, 59–60,
   62, 68, 72, 90, 91, 93, 109
   controlled release of, 84
Internalized bad objects (*continued*)
   release of, 24, 77, 133
   repression of, 22
   traumatic release of, 64–67, 69, 84,
   126, 135
Internalization (*See also* Internalized
   bad objects), 16, 21, 24, 31, 38,
   55, 59, 62, 105
   transmuting, 102–3
Introjection, 17–18, 19, 38, 54, 57

Jack, 45–48, 63, 110–12, 128–30, 140–
   41, 145
Jacobson, E., 30–32, 40
   on internalization of objects, 31
   on the ego, 31
   on the self, 31
Jeremy, 146–51

Kernberg, O., 30
Khan, M.
   on management in psychotherapy,
   88
   on the false self, 25–26
   on the true self, 25–26
Klein, M., 17–19, 20, 21, 25, 29
   on development of psychic structure, 17–19
   on maturation of object relations,
   19
   on splitting, 18–19
Kohut, H. (*See also* Self psychology),
   x, 6, 12, 24, 30, 31, 32–38, 40, 41,
   58, 60, 71, 72, 74, 80–81, 85–86,
   97–104
   on defense-resistance in psychotherapy, 6, 27, 37–38, 44, 75, 80–
   81, 97–98, 100
   on development of psychic structure, 32–38
   on confrontation in psychotherapy,
   100

on empathy, 33, 34, 44, 57, 64, 74,
   92, 97, 98–101, 102, 103, 105,
   121, 124
on goals of psychotherapy, 12, 74,
   99, 107
on idealization, 34, 35, 74, 95, 102
on internalization, 105
on interpretation and explanation
   in psychotherapy, 101, 121
on mature relationships to objects,
   34, 35
on mirroring, 34, 35, 58, 74, 95,
   102, 109
on mistakes (and optimal failures)
   in psychotherapy, 89, 101–3, 108
on narcissism, 35, 37, 52, 124
on nature of psychopathology, 34,
   36–37
on necessary qualities of the psychotherapist, 97, 103–4, 109
on negative therapeutic reaction,
   124
on process and technique in psychotherapy, 97–104, 104–5, 107
on reality ego, 36–37
on regression in psychotherapy, 98
on repression, 82, 98
on the self, 33
on self preservation, 37–38, 80–81
on selfobject transferences, 98, 99–
   100, 105, 123
on selfobjects, 34–35, 57, 58, 64, 74,
   85–86, 92, 95, 98, 99, 100, 101,
   102, 103
on splitting, 33, 36–37, 82, 98
on stages of psychotherapy, 97–99
on the therapeutic environment,
   153
on transference, 82, 85–86, 99
on transmuting internalization,
   102–3

La Planche and Pontalis, 72
Libidinal ego. (*See* Ego, Libidinal)
Lichtenstein, H., 30
Lost child, 8, 44

Meissner, W. W., 40, 48
on development of the self, 39
Mike, 137–39
Mirroring, 34, 35, 58, 74, 95, 102,
109, 112, 122, 123, 142
Mistakes and failures in psychotherapy and psychoanalysis. *See* Psychotherapy and psychoanalysis,
mistakes and failures in

Narcissism, 32, 34, 35, 37, 52, 58, 61,
62, 63, 110, 116, 124
Narcotics anonymous, 151
Negative therapeutic reaction, 77,
124–25

Object relations theory (*See also* British object relations theory, English school of object relations,
Classical analytic school of object relations), x, 12, 54
on development of psychic structure, 16–32
on psychopathology, 14

Paul, 60–61, 63, 118–20, 123–24, 126
Projection, 17–18, 19, 68, 84
Process and Technique in psychotherapy. *See* Psychotherapy and
psychoanalysis, process and
technique in
Projective identification, 42, 59
Psychic structure
characteristics of damaged self,
40–41
characteristics of healthy self, 40–
41
development of, x, 14–38, 39, 43–
44, 52, 54, 55, 67–70, 71, 72
Psychotherapists:
as good objects, 91–92, 93–94, 97,
103–4
necessary qualities of, 12, 95–97,
103–4, 109
Psychotherapy and psychoanalysis:
12

classical vs. structural approaches,
14, 29, 71–72, 74–75, 81–82, 86–
87, 104, 122–23
confrontation in, 100
defense-resistance in, 6, 27, 37–38,
44, 71, 74–81, 82, 89, 90, 91, 93,
95, 97–98, 100, 113, 124–30, 135–
42
goals of, 12, 70, 71–74, 99, 104,
107, 154–55
group, 5
interpretation and explanation in,
99, 101, 116, 121, 125, 135, 136
management in, 88–89
mistakes and failures in, 89–90,
101–3, 108, 109, 113–16, 125, 135
patient dependency in, 94–95, 100,
122–30
process and technique in, 71, 86–
104, 104–5, 107, 142
regression in, 76, 78, 83–84, 84–85,
88–89, 92–93, 96, 97, 98, 105,
118–20, 122, 123, 125, 126, 141,
146, 153
stages of, 92–93, 97–99
transference in, 65, 71, 81–86, 95, 97,
98, 99–100, 114, 122–25

Regression in psychotherapy. *See*
Psychotherapy and psychoanalysis, regression in
Regression of ego, 28, 78
Repression, 19, 20, 21, 22, 29, 37, 65,
66, 68, 69, 71, 72, 73, 76, 82, 84,
98, 117, 120, 123, 142
Rita, 52–53, 54, 56, 57, 58, 59, 74–75,
121–22, 126–27, 131–33, 139

Sam, 53–54, 55, 56, 59, 61
Schizoid phenomena, 20–23, 27–28,
30, 62, 73, 78–80, 91, 92–97, 119,
121
schizoid compromise, 79–80, 92,
93, 97, 119, 121
Self psychology (*See also* Kohut, H.),
x, 12, 24, 32, 38, 43, 44, 58, 72

Self psychology (*continued*)
  process and technique in, 87
  transference in, 122–23
  view of psychopathology, 14
Selfobject transferences, 85–86, 97,
  98, 99–100, 105, 123, 124
Selfobjects, 24, 34–35, 57, 58, 61, 64,
  67, 69, 74, 85–86, 92, 95, 97, 98,
  99, 100, 101, 102, 103, 108, 121,
  122, 125, 134, 142
  defined, 34
Splitting, 18–19, 20–23, 24, 25, 28,
  29, 30, 33, 36–37, 38, 47, 51, 60,
  61, 62–64, 67, 68, 69, 71, 72, 73,
  75, 78, 82, 83, 87, 90, 98, 104,
  111, 119, 120, 121, 123, 125, 126,
  131, 142, 144, 150, 153, 154
  vertical vs. horizontal, 37
Superego, 14, 15, 31, 32

Tom, 65–67
Transference. *See* Psychotherapy and
  psychoanalysis, transference in
True self, 25–26, 31, 38, 44, 47, 51,
  52, 60, 61, 62, 68, 70, 71, 72–73,
  75–76, 83, 87, 89, 90, 92

Wegscheider, S., x, 4, 7, 8, 9, 12
Winnicott, D.W., 12, 20, 25–27, 28,

72–73, 75–76, 78, 81, 82–84, 87,
  91, 95
  on defense-resistance in psychoth-
    erapy, 75–76, 89, 90
  on development of psychic struc-
    ture, 25–27
  on false self, 26, 43, 45, 73, 83, 87,
    89
  on goals of psychotherapy, 72–73
  on holding environment in psy-
    chotherapy, 83–84, 85, 88–89, 92,
    104
  on impingement, 76
  on management in psychotherapy,
    88–89
  on mistakes in psychotherapy: 101
  on process and technique in psy-
    chotherapy, 87–91
  on psychological health, 25
  on regression in psychotherapy,
    83–84, 85, 88–89, 92–93, 123
  on splitting, 25, 83, 87
  on transference, 82–84
  on true self, 25–26, 31, 72–73, 75–
    76, 83, 87, 89, 90, 92
Woititz, J., x, 4, 9–10, 12, 131
Wolf, S., 30, 33
Wurmser, L., 57